Cross-Cultural Research

POCKET GUIDES TO
SOCIAL WORK RESEARCH METHODS

Series Editor
Tony Tripodi, DSW
Professor Emeritus, Ohio State University

JORGE DELVA
PAULA ALLEN-MEARES
SANDRA L. MOMPER

Cross-Cultural Research

OXFORD
UNIVERSITY PRESS

2010

OXFORD

UNIVERSITY PRESS

Oxford University Press, Inc., publishes works that further
Oxford University's objective of excellence
in research, scholarship, and education.

Oxford   New York
Auckland   Cape Town   Dar es Salaam   Hong Kong   Karachi
Kuala Lumpur   Madrid   Melbourne   Mexico City   Nairobi
New Delhi   Shanghai   Taipei   Toronto

With offices in
Argentina   Austria   Brazil   Chile   Czech Republic   France   Greece
Guatemala   Hungary   Italy   Japan   Poland   Portugal   Singapore
South Korea   Switzerland   Thailand   Turkey   Ukraine   Vietnam

Copyright © 2010 by Oxford University Press, Inc.

Published by Oxford University Press, Inc.
198 Madison Avenue, New York, New York 10016

www.oup.com

Oxford is a registered trademark of Oxford University Press.

Library of Congress Cataloging-in-Publication Data

Delva, Jorge.
Cross-cultural research / by Jorge Delva, Paula Allen-Meares, Sandra L. Momper.
  p.   cm. — (Pocket guides to social work research methods)
Includes bibliographical references and index.
ISBN 978-0-19-538250-1
  1. Social service—Research—Methodology—Cross-cultural studies.
  2. Social service—Research—United States—Methodology—Cross-cultural
studies.   I. Allen-Meares, Paula, 1948–   II. Momper, Sandra L.   III. Title.
HV11.D4435 2010
001.4—dc22
2009031490

1   3   5   7   9   8   6   4   2

Printed in the United States of America
on acid-free paper

Acknowledgments

This project was supported by the National Institutes of Health (R01: DA021181; R01:DA022720), the Skillman Foundation, and the Vivian A. and James L. Curtis School of Social Work Research and Training Center. The authors are especially grateful to the Skillman Foundation for its vision and leadership and Professors Gant, Shanks, and Hollingsworth, and Project Director Patricia Miller for their review and invaluable intellectual contributions to Chapter 6. The authors also wish to thank members of the Santiago Longitudinal Study (SLS) Workgroup for their insightful discussions of the topics presented in this book. Our appreciation is also extended to University of Michigan doctoral students Ninive Sanchez and Anne Nordberg for their extensive help in editing and formatting the chapters. *Miigwetch* (thanks) to Eugene Bigboy and Isabelle Kappeler for advice on how to conduct research on a reservation and to Dr. Aurora Jackson for her commitment to and mentoring of cross-cultural researchers.

Finally, this work would not have been possible without the assistance of these colleagues and a large number of individuals and families who so graciously have opened their doors to "researchers." In the end, however, the contents of this book are solely the responsibility of the authors and do not necessarily represent the official views of the funding sources, collaborators, or study participants. All mistakes or controversial statements are solely the responsibility of the authors.

Contents

Cross-Cultural Research

1

Introduction

The purpose of this book is to provide researchers with a framework to conduct research in a culturally sensitive manner with individuals, families, and communities in diverse cultural settings in the United States, as well as in a global context. We consider cross-cultural research to be a fluid and dynamic process. Therefore, the framework we propose focuses more on the *process* than a typology of behaviors, attitudes, values, and beliefs by which cross-cultural research can be successful. This process is based on our real-life research experiences with diverse populations in the United States and other countries. We purposely do not offer a menu (typology) of behaviors, beliefs, values, and attitudes about specific populations that readers can use to understand different cultures. In other words, readers will not find a table with columns (list of different populations) and rows (list of attributes) and cells with a check mark that indicates whether a cultural group fits that attribute. Rather, in this book we offer a process that researchers conducting cross-cultural research (or, for that matter, any type of research) can use to increase their chances of success. We think that a detailed discussion of process is more important than a presentation of prescribed steps because it allows readers to adapt this information to their own unique circumstances.

CROSS-CULTURAL RESEARCH IN SOCIAL WORK AND OTHER DISCIPLINES

Definitions of cross-cultural research vary considerably and are generally adapted from the anthropological and psychological disciplines. In this book, we define cross-cultural research as a natural experiment involving cultural groups in which the researcher is interested in existing relationships among variables under circumstances where these variables have been modified by cultural conditions (Brislin, 1983; Guthrie & Lonner, 1986; Triandis et al., 1980).

Historically cross-cultural research compared results across cultures, with the dominant culture frequently being the referent culture. Ideally, cross-cultural research that integrates the "emic" approach, in which the culture is studied from within with constructs specific to that culture, and the "etic" approach, in which the culture is studied from without and compared across cultures highlighting more universal constructs, is desirable in social science research (Canino, Lewis-Fernandez, & Bravo, 1997). As a side note, we find it fascinating that the now well-known "emic" and "etic" concepts were first coined by a linguist, Kenneth Pike (Pike, 1967), a point that highlights the central role that language plays in cross-cultural research. The critical importance of language in conducting cross-cultural research is demonstrated in several chapters. Readers interested in learning more about the history and controversies surrounding these concepts are encouraged to read Pike's original work (1967) and the book on the same topic by Headland, Pike, and Harris (1990).

In cross-cultural research it is important to be culturally sensitive to the racial, ethnic, and cultural characteristics, experiences, norms, values, behavioral patterns, and beliefs of the people one is studying (Fukuyama, 1990; Pinderhughes, 1989; Resnicow, Braithwaite, Ahluwalia, & Baranowski, 1999). It is also important to incorporate into the research activity knowledge of relevant historical, environmental, and social forces that make up the cultural background and cultural reality of the study participants.

Cultural sensitivity is an ongoing and open-ended series of substantive and methodological insertions and adaptations designed to mesh the process of inquiry with the ethno-cultural characteristics of the group being studied (Pena & Koss-Chioino, 1992; Rogler, 1989). For example, it is ideal for a researcher to involve participants from the beginning, even before the research question is conceptualized. This can help the researcher be more cognizant of his or her own values and beliefs and how these can influence the choice of research questions, methods, and interpretations (Matsumoto, 1994; Mohatt et al., 2004; Montero, 1994; Orlandi, Weston, & Epstein, 1992). Engaging with community leaders early on, hiring community members, participating in community events, respecting the culture of the community, and giving back to the community (in ways that the members prefer) are all important components of cultural sensitivity. Cultural sensitivity in cross-cultural research helps researchers gather more valid data because the relationship with participants is based on "where they are." We posit that this understanding increases the likelihood that the researcher can accurately assess a social problem and thereby assist individuals, families, and communities in implementing effective solutions.

We are concerned with what appears to be a tendency for researchers studying different population groups to label a behavior, belief, value, or attitude as a cultural characteristic when in fact any of these could be reflections of other identities, or at the very least a combination of various identities. Some of these identities might be income level, wealth, educational level, occupational status, racial and ethnic makeup, sex, gender, sexual identity, immigration and intergenerational status, religion, among others. We are also concerned that in an attempt to be culturally sensitive, researchers can make sweeping generalizations and attach labels to groups studied that may be not only incorrectly attributed to culture but also that are static and take on essentialist characteristics. For example, referring to groups as "religious and/or spiritual," "fatalistic or future oriented," "individually or collectively oriented," or "family centered" results in essentialist models of groups of individuals that are simplistic, fixed, ahistorical, and apolitical. We realize that the practice of labeling groups in this manner has political implications. From a dominant population perspective (i.e., a colonial power, a majority group), these sweeping generalizations (i.e., our group values "organization," "reflection," "hard work") serve to reaffirm their dominance. On the other hand, for populations that have experienced unequal treatment and oppression, many of these sweeping generalizations serve to devalue them and further reinforce their subjugated position. However, the use of labels with a cultural attribution is not a phenomenon observed only among dominant cultures. Groups that are or consider themselves oppressed also use labels to make fun of and devalue the dominant "culture," while at the same time using labels that are self-derogatory. We try to avoid sweeping generalizations of the populations we study. Occasionally we make generalized statements about populations, but we also present considerable evidence to support these statements.

As an illustration of the problem with cultural labels, we use the "fatalistic" label that is often assigned to Hispanics and that appears in well-intended cross-cultural texts. It is not uncommon for these texts to label Hispanics as having a "fatalistic" orientation to life as opposed to the optimism and drive to overcome life's obstacles assigned to Anglos. These statements are based on research that compares how Hispanics' and Anglos' answers to items on a measure that purports to assess the construct of "fatalism" differ. Results of these studies generally show that Hispanics score higher on these items, leading researchers to label Hispanics as having a more fatalistic perception of life. Although we do not disagree that there are differences on how different populations may endorse a selection of items about worldviews, we take issue with the labeling that results from it. If one considers what Latin American immigrants (whether legal or illegal) go through to establish themselves in the United States (and this goes for any immigrant anywhere in the world), one is hard pressed to think of Hispanics as being "fatalistic" and not "goal and future oriented." On the contrary, it takes a substantially optimistic individual, one who dreams of a better future for himself or herself and his or her children, to endure the challenges, sometimes life threatening, of moving to another country. Hence, labeling Hispanics as "fatalistic" is not only incorrect, but it also does not truly serve to understand the distribution of the diversity of experiences of Hispanics and of all other populations in the world. Similarly, the research that describes the double standards in male–female relationships among Hispanics with such labels as "marianismo" and "machismo" tends to (a) freeze discussions of gender behaviors into a false dichotomy ignoring the distributions (ranges) of these behaviors, (b) ignore their manifestation as a function of their intersection with the distribution of other identities (i.e., intergenerational status, country of origin), and (c) make it seem that these double standards only exist among Hispanics. One can make similar arguments concerning the use of other labels commonly utilized to distinguish individuals from different cultural backgrounds. To better illustrate our point, we include a hypothetical graphical representation of the distribution of behaviors, attitudes,

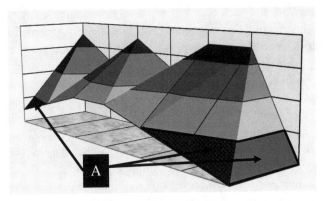

Figure 1.1 Hypothetical distributions of behaviors, attitudes, values, and beliefs as a function of cultural elements and other identities, including their intersections.

values, and beliefs that individuals, families, and communities may have as a function of cultural elements and those of other identities (i.e., immigration status, age, gender, sexual and gender identity, religion, racial and ethnic background, educational level, and occupational status), including their intersections (see Fig. 1.1). If we assume that fatalistic scores are represented by the dark gray portion of the graph (see area labeled 'A'), we can see that the distribution of these scores (averages, medians, standard deviations, range, etc…) will vary according to where one positions oneself in the graph.

Even if the fatalism label were valid, our understanding of this construct may vary depending on the perspective one takes when examining it. Broad statements about it can result in simplistic, static, stereotypical, and uninformative views about populations. Furthermore, we suggest that rather than making broad statements about Hispanics and Anglos or any other group by simply comparing average scores on a "fatalistic" measure, it is much more informative to study how individuals who differ in a measure of "fatalism" may also differ on some outcome (i.e., how variation in this measure is associated with variations in engagement with mental-health providers). In other words, we suggest that an in-depth investigation of how these variables are associated, and how this association may or may not vary according to the individuals' other identities (immigration status, nationality, acculturation, sexual and gender identity, education, occupation, wealth, individual and family income, race and ethnicity, and so forth), will result in richer, more accurate, and precise information that can better inform the delivery of mental-health treatment, something that sweeping generalizations about groups cannot accomplish. From this perspective, understanding how one group scores on a measure relative to another group is informative. However, it is more important to understand how fatalism among people seeking mental-health treatment is related to increased treatment retention, and to investigate how the magnitude and direction of this association may differ as a function of being Hispanic or Anglo, including its variation as a function of other identities (e.g., immigration status).

In summary, we are concerned with the common practice of improperly attributing to *culture*—those behaviors, beliefs, values, and attitudes that if examined more carefully may be the result of the shared influences of gender, socioeconomic status, immigration status, racial and ethnic backgrounds. Likewise, we also call on researchers whose focus is mainly on studying other identities (i.e., gender, immigration, sexual, etc) to include a cross-cultural perspective in their work and to consider the multiple identities individuals experience. This acknowledgment of the resulting complexity of an individual or group of individuals is not intended for social work researchers and practitioners to throw their hands up in despair and give up attempting to understand why people behave the way they do, finding ways to influence behavior, and understanding variations between groups. We argue against the use of broad stereotypical statements. We encourage researchers to explain behaviors in terms of their various distributions, with valleys and peaks that intersect in multiple and complex ways (as shown in Fig. 1.1).

PURPOSE AND ORGANIZATION OF THE BOOK

We describe the application of our conceptual framework to various research methods that researchers may utilize to conduct research that falls within the following three aims:

1. To understand and describe the nature and extent to which a particular problem occurs
2. To understand the etiology or potential factors associated with the occurrence of a particular problem

3. To evaluate programs or interventions designed to ameliorate or eliminate a problem

These three research aims tend to encompass most of the work in which researchers in social work and social and epidemiological sciences engage. Furthermore, these aims are sufficiently broad to allow different research methods to be used as examples. Through this work we seek to describe unique methodological issues one faces when conducting research with cross-cultural populations.

We rely on our extensive research experiences to illustrate our approach to studying diverse cultural groups using a variety of research methods. For each set of research aims listed earlier, we describe what guided the formulation of the research question(s), the theoretical model, and the development and implementation of the project. As you may have experienced with your own research projects, each of the projects we describe includes a tremendous amount of preparatory work and implementation activities, some of which are somewhat unique to a project while others cut across. Because of the extensive amount of information available for each project, we thought it would be more informative for the reader if we highlighted some key aspects of each project rather than describing all of the details. The key aspects we selected are based on the belief that these are considerably important and that they could serve to inform a project the reader may plan to develop. Certainly, all pieces of a research project are essential to its success. In narrowing our focus to selected aspects of a project, the intention is not to minimize the importance of the components that are not discussed. Rather, the focus on particular aspects stems from our knowledge of the field and the belief that the information we share will be of practical use to researchers. Of course, these selections are also informed by our own professional interests of the topics we discuss.

We would like to introduce three caveats of this book. First, we are very cautious not to inappropriately generalize the application of a particular research method with a particular population to other groups. For example, conducting mixed-methods research with American Indian populations living in the Northeast on rural reservations is not like conducting the same research with individuals living in other regions and countries. It is impossible to cover how one research method would be applied to all the cultural groups that exist in the

United States (not to speak of the rest of the world) and equally impossible to discuss various research method. We are also very careful when making cultural attributions for the reasons presented earlier in this chapter.

The primary purpose of this book is different from that of standard research methods books, whose function is to cover research methods in substantial depth and breadth, and from books about cross-cultural populations that provide considerable detail about diverse populations. Sometimes these texts provide overly simplistic generalizations of behaviors, resulting in stereotypical labels. We offer very specific, concrete, feasible examples of some aspect of a research method as applied to a diverse population with which we are intimately familiar. Our familiarity with a particular population and research method allows us to provide detailed descriptions of the process. Our wish is that researchers will gain insights into designing their own studies with their particular populations.

Second, despite our extensive experience conducting research with diverse populations in the United States and in other countries, we do not profess absolute knowledge of the populations we have studied and worked with—although we have considerable expertise on those research methods we describe. Also note that, with the exception of Chapter 2 on American Indians who live on rural reservations, all other chapters focus on populations living in urban areas. Hence, most of the cross-cultural research experiences we describe in this book focus on populations living in large cities. Therefore, we do not have empirical evidence on the extent to which our urban experiences can translate to nonurban populations (except for Chapter 2).

Additionally, the examples we describe fall into different points of the emic–etic continuum, with some studies taking a more emic perspective (i.e., Chapter 2), others presenting more of an etic approach (i e., Chapter 3), and yet others presenting an emic–etic distinction that is less salient (i.e., Chapters 4–6). For example, in Chapter 2 we highlight a number of steps taken to conduct research with American Indians living on a rural reservation. Emphasis is placed on a number of cultural elements that researchers are advised to take into consideration. Using these specific examples with American Indians, we also take the opportunity to highlight commonalities with the other populations we present in this book (universal considerations), even though the cultural elements (the specific aspects of a population) may differ. For example, the gatekeeping role among American Indians on rural reservations falls into the hands of the tribal leader and tribal council (Chapter 2), while that role for the student populations studied in Central America (Chapter 3) fell into the hands of the corresponding Ministries of Health or Ministries of Education, among others, as well as with the corresponding school superintendents, principals, and teachers. On the other hand, the gatekeeping role among the families participating in a longitudinal study of drug use in Santiago, Chile, fell into the hands of a well-known and trusted health and medical research institute, the University of Chile Institute of Nutrition and Technology of Foods (INTA, in Spanish) (Chapter 4).

Third, even though we try to stay abreast of cutting-edge developments on research methods and cross-cultural practices, we have not included all innovations that are underway, especially if they are implemented in fields outside ours. We believe that the best research comes from multidisciplinary and interdisciplinary teams and is informed by the study participants. In our chapters we highlight these critical aspects. We also humbly acknowledge that there are times we have made mistakes: when we have not implemented the research methods in their ideal formats, or when we could have conducted projects in a more culturally sensitive manner. Throughout the chapters we discuss these instances, thanks to the benefit of hindsight. We constantly aspire to learn from our mistakes, implementing the best research methods and trying to be as culturally aware as possible—all of which can only be accomplished with the help of our dedicated collaborators.

SIGNIFICANCE FOR SOCIAL WORK RESEARCH

As we indicated earlier, in this book we describe and discuss the application of different research methods with various population groups for three types of research aims or areas social work researchers and others generally investigate. The various examples of research projects implemented with different groups will provide the reader with a comprehensive overview of the implementation of different research methods in a culturally appropriate manner with diverse cultural groups. In addition, all of the projects described have received some type of funding either from the National Institutes of Health, private foundations, or university seed funds. We highlight this point about funding because we believe it is important to communicate to our colleagues that it is not only possible to receive funding, some of it quite large indeed, but also that it is imperative that such funding be obtained in order to better study the complexities of cross-cultural research. It is the authors' experiences that such funding allows for more comprehensive work, including a broader range of collaborators, than when funding is not available. Furthermore, given the complexity of the problems, strong emphasis is placed on the need to conduct cross-cultural research with multidisciplinary and/or interdisciplinary teams. *We strongly believe that multiple epistemologies and methodologies are needed to inform the conduct of cross-cultural research.* However, exactly because of the diverse perspectives that this type of work generates, a substantial amount of time must be spent by these teams to learn and value each other's languages, methods, and cultures, as noted by the joint report on interdisciplinary research by the National Academy of Sciences, National Academy of Engineering, and Institute of Medicine.[1]

We sincerely hope that after reading this book, researchers will feel more encouraged to form partnerships with diverse population groups (and this includes study participants and researchers from other disciplines) in order to conduct research that will serve to fill important-knowledge gaps. Too often researchers are reluctant to conduct research or even think aboutconducting research with some populations, even though these populations would welcome such collaboration if the work is a partnership and conducted in a culturally informed manner.

We reiterate that the research methods we describe in this book fall under one of the following three research aims: *(1)* to understand and describe the nature and extent to which a particular problem occurs; *(2)* to understand the etiology or potential factors associated with the occurrence of a problem; and *(3)* to evaluate programs or interventions designed to ameliorate or eliminate a problem. Under the first research aim we cover two topics, one on mixed-methods research and one on population-based surveys. We begin the discussion of research methods by focusing on mixed-methods research because we strongly believe that multiple methods, multiple ways of knowing, are indeed essential to better understand the complexity of human and organizational behaviors. Chapter 2, entitled "Conducting Mixed-Methods Research: An

Illustration with American Indians in the United States," presents considerable details about important cultural elements investigators should take into consideration when working with American Indian populations living in rural reservations. This work relies heavily on an emic perspective. In Chapter 3, entitled "Conducting Large-Scale Population-Based Survey Research," we provide an example of a large multicountry survey of drug use, a study that was conducted following primarily an etic approach. From this study we highlight some key components of survey research that researchers may find useful when planning large population surveys, whether these are implemented in schools, organizations, cities, counties, states, or countries.

The topic covered under the second research aim is on designing and implementing longitudinal studies. Chapter 4 is entitled "Conducting Longitudinal Studies." In this section we provide an example of two large longitudinal studies designed to prospectively investigate associations between variables of interest. One study is underway in an international setting and the other in a large cosmopolitan city in the United States. These studies offer unique insights about large longitudinal studies. These studies were guided with a mix of an emic–etic lens. Finally, the two topics covered under the third research aim focus on the design of a large randomized clinical trial in a community setting and the conduct of community-based participatory research. The corresponding chapters are entitled "Use of Experimental Designs in Community Settings" (Chapter 5) and "Conducting Community-Based Participatory Research" (Chapter 6). The chapter on experimental designs provides an in-depth description of the planning and implementation of a large randomized clinical trial in a community setting. This study's focus, using both an emic and etic approach, became increasingly centered around socioeconomic elements as opposed to what we anticipated would be more of a cultural lens. As we describe later in the chapter, the success of this project became critically dependent on being sensitive to the socioeconomic conditions of the population. We then conclude our presentation of research methods with a discussion of community-based participatory research using as an example a large study presently underway in the City of Detroit. From these two studies we believe researchers will be able to draw important inferences to inform their particular studies. Finally, in Chapter 7, we conclude our book with a brief discussion and summary of the material presented and propose what may be a novel idea: for cross-cultural researchers to seriously consider incorporating an intersectionality lens into their work. Briefly, intersectionality refers to the need to consider the multiple identities that define people and that in turn people create, resulting in individuals whose entire selves are more than the sum of their parts. The implication of this concept for cross-cultural research is discussed in Chapter 7.

We believe this book will contribute to researchers' desire and ability to conduct research in a more culturally sensitive and appropriate manner, resulting in better knowledge that can be used to improve the lives of the populations we work with. This book will be of special interest to social work faculty, social work researchers, doctoral students, doctoral seminars, as well as a companion text for Master of Social Work (MSW) research and evaluation methods courses. The book should also be of interest to allied professions and disciplines such as psychology, education, sociology, public health, and anthropology.

This book was written with the specific purpose of reaching a broad spectrum of readers with diverse cultural and research interests. Given that this book is on the intersection of culture and research methods, several chapters include considerable cultural details and other chapters present a more methodological focus. These details may be too advanced for some, adequate for others, and too simple for those with advanced knowledge of the particular subject matter. Nonetheless, we hope our experiences will help others develop cross-cultural projects that are just as (or even more) interesting and helpful in improving people's quality of life as the projects we have conducted. It is in this spirit that we write about our experiences.

2

Conducting Mixed-Methods Research: An Illustration With American Indians in the United States

The application of mixed methods is becoming an increasingly recognized methodology to better understand a particular problem or study a research question. In mixed-methods research, the researcher collects, analyzes, and integrates quantitative and qualitative data in a single study or in multiple studies in a sustained program of inquiry (Creswell, 2003). Recent books by Creswell (2003), Johnson and Christensen (2004), and Tashakkori and Teddlie (2003) provide considerable information on the methodology of mixed-methods research designs. Creswell (2003) identifies three mixed-methods designs:

1. *Explanatory*. The researcher prioritizes the quantitative data collection and analysis and collects the quantitative data first. The qualitative data are subsequently collected for the purpose of refining and enriching the results of the quantitative data.

2. *Exploratory.* The researcher emphasizes the qualitative data collection and analysis and collects the qualitative data first. The quantitative data are subsequently collected to build on or explain the qualitative results.

3. *Triangulation.* The researcher collects both quantitative and qualitative data concurrently and gives equal priority to both. The results are compared to determine whether the two sets of data are similar or dissimilar.

Mixed-methods research provides the opportunity to collect data to explain the strength of relationships, make predictions, and to "study things in their natural settings . . . to make sense of or interpret phenomenon in terms of the meanings people bring to them" (Denzin & Lincoln, 2000, p. 3). Mixed-methods research is particularly important for researchers who are trying to conduct research in a way that bridges the gap between a dominant culture and diverse cultural groups.

We utilize two studies to describe the application of mixed-methods research. Study 1 was an explanatory study of the intersection of maternal gambling, parenting, self-efficacy, depression, social supports, and child behavior problems among American Indians living on a rural Midwestern reservation (Momper & Jackson, 2007). Quantitative data were gathered first from a total of 150 women, and then a subgroup of 20 women participated in a semi-structured interview. This study received funding from the National Institutes of Mental Health (NIMH), the Newberry Library, and the University of Pittsburgh's Provost Development Funds. Next we explain how data received from this study, the initial explanatory study, led to a second study, hereafter referred to as Study 2, on gambling, alcohol, smoking, and drug use on the reservation. In Study 2, eight focus groups were conducted as "talking circles" (2006 and 2007) with 49 participants between the ages of 12 and 78 (Momper, Delva, & Reed, in press). This study received funding from the National Institute of Drug Abuse and the University of Michigan Tobacco Research Network. This chapter uses information from both studies to illustrate the design and implementation of mixed-methods research in a culturally sensitive manner.

As indicated in the Introduction, in this and subsequent chapters we describe what guided the formulation of the research question(s) and what theoretical model was used, and we provide examples of the development and implementation of the project. In addition to these three topics, we highlight at least two critical aspects of the projects that we believe readers may find useful in planning their own projects because they would be indicators of the extent to which a researcher is sensitive to the cultural and historical aspects of American Indians' lives. First, we emphasize the necessity of being a cultural broker for the Indian community. Cultural brokering is the act of bridging, linking, or mediating between groups or persons of different cultural backgrounds for the purpose of reducing conflict or producing change (Jezewski, 1990). A cultural broker can be defined as a go-between, one who advocates on behalf of another individual or a group of people (Jezewski & Sotnik, 2001). Second, we describe in detail access issues as well as issues surrounding differences between researchers, whether Indian or not Indian, and the Indians participating in the research. The researcher has to be willing and open to recognizing those differences and to question critically his or her own worldview or paradigm and make the necessary adjustments. For example, the researcher needs to reassess his or her predetermined beliefs about competence based on formal education alone because many individuals without formal education can offer tremendous insight into the research process. The insight can be acquired through other ways of knowing, such as through cultural experiences and an oral tradition of learning. Another example relates to concerns about following a timeline and meeting deadlines, especially if funding is involved and the funding sources require that "deliverables" be turned in on time for accountability purposes. However, in many cultures, the concept of time is more fluid and less important than building and establishing trusting relationships. It is important for the researcher to learn to navigate these conflicting demands to be successful when conducting research not only with American Indians but also with other populations.

The researcher also needs to recognize the importance of family and tribal community when conducting the research. For example, if a tribal member "walks on", or "crosses over the river" (i.e., dies) during the course of the study, the researcher must be willing to reschedule appointments. Or if a participant's family member becomes ill and that participant needs to be at the hospital with the family member, the researcher needs to accept this as a component of Indian culture. Being an active participant in the community of the reservation is imperative as well, for example, being willing to help with the preparation of the feast for the person who has walked on or to give the participant a ride to the hospital to see the family member who is ill, if needed. As we indicate in Chapter 1, we prefer not to offer a typology of behaviors researchers should follow when conducting cross-cultural research. The specific illustrations presented above are meant to be treated as a few examples of things to look for when working with American Indians; they in no way represent a comprehensive list. These examples are for the purpose of illustrating what a culturally sensitive researcher—one that is open to learning and to new experiences—may become aware of when working with American Indians in order to adjust his or her behavior accordingly. Below we proceed with a description of the study on the intersection of maternal gambling, parenting, self-efficacy, depression, social supports, and child behavior problems among American Indians living on a reservation.

THE RESEARCH QUESTIONS AND THEORETICAL MODEL (STUDY 1)

Research Questions

A researcher who is sensitive to American Indians' experiences is aware of the long history of distrust that exists between American Indians and the general population, including the research community. Therefore, the researcher will be more likely to include the input of Indian people from the very beginning of the project. In this study, the conceptualization of the idea for studying the gambling behaviors of American Indian women came from a conversation that took place between the American Indian researcher (co-author Momper) and a young Indian man who said, "If you are going to do a study of Indians, why don't you study my mom and auntie's gambling?" This comment led to discussions with Indian elders and a meeting with tribal council members about the impact of gambling on this reservation.

Previous research on Indian gaming, which was legalized in 1988 with the passage of the Indian Gaming Regulatory Act (IGRA), indicates that problem gambling among American Indians has increased, especially among women (Costello, Compton, Keeler, & Angold, 2003; IGRA, 1988; Volberg & Abbott, 1997). Additionally in a North Dakota comparison study of gambling, the lifetime pathological and problematic gambling rate in the Indian population was found to be 14.5% compared to 3.5% in the general population (Cozzetto & Larocque, 1996). Hence, a collaborative decision was made to study the gambling behaviors of Indian women to determine whether their gambling behaviors were affecting them and their families. In 2004 a mixed-method study of the gambling behaviors of 150 American Indian women was conducted on a Midwestern reservation. The women ($N = 150$) completed a self-administered questionnaire with standardized measures, and a subgroup of 20 women consented to be qualitatively interviewed by the researcher, a tribally enrolled member of the reservation. In this study, four questions were addressed (Momper & Jackson, 2007 *(1)* Is maternal gambling associated with American Indian children's behavioral functioning? *(2)* Are access to helpful social support and more adequate parenting in the home environment associated with children's behavioral functioning in American Indian families in which mothers gamble? *(3)* Is the effect of maternal gambling on children's behavioral functioning moderated by the mothers' access to helpful social support and more adequate parenting in the home environment? *(4)* Is the child's gender a factor in the relationships between maternal gambling and parenting and children's behavioral functioning? In the study there also was interest in the mothers' perceptions of financial strain because even though the casino has helped this tribe gain revenue, the tribe remains the poorest in the state (Jensen-DeHart, 1999).

Theoretical Model

The theoretical model that guided the work was the ecological theoretical perspective comprising microsystems, mesosystems, exosystems, and macrosystems (Bronfenbrenner & Ceci, 1994). American Indians practice balance in their ecosystems and place a great deal of importance on human ecology through tribal structures, clan formation, and family interdependence (Good Tracks, 1973; Joe, 1989; Red Horse, 1980). More explicitly, American Indian children are born into two relational systems: a biological family and a kinship network, such as a clan or band

(Blanchard & Barsh, 1980). The first of these consists of a microsystem (e.g., the home environment and family relationships); the second, a mesosystem consisting of processes between or among two or more microsystems, both of which contain the child (e.g., the home environment and the kinship network). An exosystem consists of processes between or among two or more settings, only one of which contains the child (e.g., the home environment is a microsystem involving both the child and the mother, whereas the gambling casino is a setting involving the mother, but not the child). In this study, influences of the broader cultural or socioeconomic environments—that is, the macrosystem—include the Indian Gaming Regulatory Act (IGRA) and the reservation casino. In the next section we discuss how the project came to be.

Project Implementation

Before discussing this process, the following story is offered as an example of a dilemma encountered by the author of the study while sharing the genesis of this project.

> When I was young my great uncle, who was a Chief, took me on a walk through the woods to observe the behaviors of an older bear in hibernation. While walking on a trail in the woods he told me about walks he took with international students from a local university who were interested in Indian history and hiking on the reservation on "old Indian trails." I was excited and impressed that he had been doing this for students and told him. Then he said, "My girl, I never took them on a real 'old Indian trail' I just made them believe that it was one."

The story represents a dilemma for the author, an American Indian researcher, because the concern is about how much "insider" knowledge should be shared about accessing American Indian cultures. On the other hand, as a social worker, the author believes there is an obligation to add to the knowledge base about other cultures. Thus, this section proposes to do that: to inform researchers in social work and in other professions about how this project came to be while at the same time being sensitive that some information must remain private. Readers need to keep in mind, however, that this information about cultural factors is intended to serve as a guide and should be adapted, with input from tribal members, if used on other Indian reservations or in urban Indian communities. The hope is that this information will assist social workers and others who want to conduct research with American Indians to be more culturally informed in the design, collection, analysis, and reporting of results.

Proposing the Study to the Academic/Research Community

If you are an academic researcher, the time will come when you and the tribal members will have to propose the work to the academic/research community (i.e., writing a proposal to seek funding, submitting an Institutional Review Board [IRB] application). At this point in the research process you become the cultural broker who bridges the gap that exists between the tribal community and the academic community. You are in a dual position here, as you may be a doctoral student, or a researcher, who is also a member of the academic community while at the same time a broker for the Indian people. This is where you must represent the "voices" of the Indians, which have too often been silenced. If you are able to do this, you will gain the trust of the Indians. For example, in this study concerns were raised about the informed consent process. Some of the questions raised were as follows: "How are you going to gain access?" "Is it hard to get information from Indians, especially Indians on reservations?" "Why do you want to study Indian gambling—why not study drinking instead?" These comments were evidence of the need for researchers who are Indian and not Indian to conduct studies on reservations to illuminate Indian people's needs and overcome misconceptions about Indians and research. Access can occur, Indians do want to tell their stories, Indian drinking studies have been done, and few Indian gambling studies have been conducted. This study was important to the Indians, and as a social work researcher and cultural broker, the goal was to convince the academic community of the importance of the study. Indian people value education and knowledge, are receptive to research that includes and values them in the process, and were pleased to assist the researcher. At this point, it is important to note that one does not have to be Indian or know everything there is about Indians to conduct research with them. What is critical is understanding and being sensitive to the needs of marginalized populations.

Human Subjects Protection

As a member of the academic/research community, IRB approval from the University had to be obtained before the study could be conducted. Additionally, for the University a written letter from the tribe stating that they approved of the study and would allow the conduct of the study on the reservation with tribal members was necessary. Some tribes now have their own tribal review boards that meet on a regular basis and decide on research studies on their reserves; this tribe did not, so tribal approval was received from the tribal council. Once this verbal approval was received, a proposal was drafted for the study as well as an application for an NIMH dissertation award to receive funds to assist in completing the study.

Obtaining Tribal Permission/Consent

This is one of the most important steps in the research process, as the researcher needs to build a "face-to-face" relationship with tribal members. This involves spending time on the reservation with tribal community members. For example, prior to the conduct of the study, attend events like powwows that occur on or near the reservation; volunteer with the youth, or with the elderly; or set up meetings with people on the reservation who are social workers or providers of social services to tribal members. However, your participation has to be genuine, not just to conduct the study. Be sensitive to differences in race, ethnicity, gender, age, education, and socioeconomic status during these times. Additionally, be cognizant of the history of the particular tribe and be interested in the history if an elder chooses to share it with you. Also be willing to share your history, as it does not make sense to an Indian person to be involved in a research study where he or she is answering personal questions yet does not know who you are (Napoli, 1999). Additionally, if you are a researcher who is not Indian, you need to build a relationship with a tribal member who is preferably an elder who can act as a liaison with the tribal council and tribal members. Building this type of relationship involves time—time that is not only spent on the study and the researcher's needs but also on interacting, helping, and following the lead of the elder (e.g., telling her or him about you and your family, giving her or him a ride, babysitting, attending feasts, or burials, etc.). As we describe in other chapters, being culturally sensitive and gaining access to other populations also involves a process of sharing and giving back, though the specific ways by which one shares or gives back may vary across populations. The point here is that a culturally sensitive researcher approaches populations with an open mind and actively sets out to look for clues that will indicate what behaviors are appropriate and will be appreciated by the populations in order to develop trust and access.

If you are planning on conducting research on a reservation that has its own tribal IRB, you will need to contact them. However, the best way to do this is to also establish a face-to-face relationship with a tribal member who can tell tribal IRB review members about you and about your study prior to your proposal being submitted to them for review. This will enable an insider to vouch for you and to support your project. In the study reported here the author spent time talking with a female tribal elder to learn about current activities on the reservation and how to accomplish the study in a culturally appropriate manner, as the author had not lived on the reservation for several years. Ideas were shared and then the elder advised the author to talk to the tribal chairman to get permission to conduct the study.

The author was located off the reservation, so a call to the tribal chairman's office was made and a meeting was set up with him for a time when the author would be on the reservation. The author realized later that setting up a time was not effective in Indian culture. A meeting had to occur in a more casual way, for example, just walking down the hallway, or going from one meeting to the next, or stopping by informally to talk about family and then discuss the study. When the author arrived for the meeting, the tribal chairman was not in his office, but she was told where he was and proceeded to find him. A researcher has to introduce himself or herself before discussing the study with the chairman. The tribal chairman already knew the author and her family. For a researcher who is not Indian, who has already spent time on the reservation and attended tribal events, the tribal chairman would have already seen you around and would recognize you. If you have not previously spent sufficient time on the reservation interacting with

Indians, this is the point where you will know that they are not ready to accept or trust you. Even the author had to remind him about who she was, her relationship to the tribal elder, and her family members. Also, instead of racing headlong into the planned speech about the study, she had to take the time to listen to him and answer questions about how her family was doing. In other words, she had to slow down and discuss the more important aspects of life. Once verbal approval was received, we continued to talk about members of the younger generation who were presently in school and how important school has been for them and for the tribe. The key to this meeting and discussion was not that the study was the most important thing but that the researcher was willing to interact and self-disclose information so that a trusting relationship could be built. The author mistakenly thought that this verbal approval was going to be enough for the University IRB because it was enough for the tribe. In the next section we describe the additional steps taken for IRB approval to take place.

Cultural Brokering or Negotiating Two Worlds

As a researcher in Indian country, one has to be able to negotiate the "world of academia" and the "world of the reservation" with particular attention to safeguarding Indian culture. As social work researchers, we are charged with protecting participants from harm. When conducting research on a reservation, this is particularly important yet difficult. The difference between the academic culture and Indian culture on a reservation is vast. A researcher in Indian country needs to be able to recognize these differences and guard against imposing the rules of the academic culture on the Indian culture. Additionally, both Indian and non-Indian researchers need to be activists in terms of teaching academia about the cultural differences and suggesting ways to close the gap. In this study when the proposal and NIMH documents were complete, the verbal approval of the tribal chairman was not sufficient to satisfy University IRB requirements, and written approval was necessary.

The author of the study undergoes a continuous internal struggle as she attempts to meet both the expectations of the academic world and the world of the reservation. Indian people have historically relied on oral tradition (Ambler, 1995; Montejo, 1994), yet this is not the case with universities; for instance, the word of the tribal chairman was good enough for the tribe and the author, but in order to conduct this study, the author was forced to meet standard written IRB requirements. The tribal chairman and vice-tribal chairman were contacted, via the telephone and mail, to obtain written approval. After weeks of attempting this method, a face-to-face meeting was scheduled again. The author traveled to the reservation (900 miles), went to the tribal administration building to say "hi" to relatives, and saw the vice-tribal chairman. He then walked her to the tribal chairman's office and told him of her need for this written letter of approval. The tribal chairman invited her to the full tribal council meeting that was about to begin. Without advance notice of this meeting, she was unprepared and faced the embarrassment of standing in front of the full tribal council dressed in shorts and a t-shirt as she presented the proposal to the council members. Council members first wanted to know about her connections to the reservation. Once connections were established, and the vice-chairman vouched for her, the council members were supportive of the study. Ultimately, the tribal secretary formulated the letter and sent it to the author. If you are not Indian, you can draw from relationships already established by your presence on the reservation to make connections with tribal leaders. Once again a face-to-face meeting was expected to develop trust. It did not matter to them how she was dressed to present this proposal; what mattered was how she was as a person, who her family and friends were, her reservation connections, and so forth.

A researcher who is not Indian needs to be aware that Indians are often very nonmaterialistic and base their view of a person on personal characteristics and values, not their economic standing (Attneave, 1969). For the researcher who is not Indian, the liaison with the elder tribal member and the participation in tribal events will be the entree, and acceptance into, the tribal community. Tribal members will vouch for you. Of note is that later when the author was conducting another study on the reservation, tribal participants asked about IRB issues and the lengthy consent form. A participant questioned why the forms had so many pages and then said, "Don't those white people trust each other?"

Hiring Tribal Members

The training and employment of tribal members as research staff or assistants is a necessary step toward adequately conducting a study with a reservation (Caldwell et al., 2005). American Indian staff residing on the reservation will be preferred by reservation residents. This is parallel to hiring locals when conducting research with other populations, as illustrated in the other chapters as well. The relationship between the researcher and the tribal participants has to be a two-way relationship. For example, the research assistant or other tribal employee can be introduced to the academic world, and in turn he or she can introduce the researcher to the world of the reservation. In this study an elder tribal member was hired as a research assistant (RA). At this point in the hiring process the researcher must be aware of his or her own biases in terms of hiring persons with degrees (Stubben, 2001). Elders possess cultural, spiritual, and experiential knowledge that is highly valued and respected. The RA was a female tribal elder who came from a prominent family, had lots of experience with tribal politics, had assisted others in conducting surveys, and had status in the tribe. Hiring someone from the tribe benefits the tribe and the person, economically, and allows her or him to acquire research skills. For example, as a result of the RA's participation in this study, she went to enroll in the tribal community college to acquire computer skills. Subsequently, she ended up enrolling full time and recently graduated with an associate's degree. The empowerment of the RA is an example of the positive change that can occur through the research process (Tinkler, 2004). Similar situations have arisen with staff in the other projects we describe later. For example, a number of African American staff in the randomized clinical trial described in Chapter 5 went on to complete their undergraduate or graduate degrees.

Simultaneously, the researcher's benefit from this relationship was that the RA served as the entrée to the Indian women. Because the author had not lived on the reservation since she was a young child, the RA vouched for her and deemed her to be "trustworthy"; as a result, the women accepted her and participated in the study. The RA taught her more about Indian culture and what is important in life from an Indian perspective. When the study was completed, they attended a conference to introduce the RA to the academic community and to present the results of the study. This exemplifies how culturally sensitive research benefits everyone in the partnership. Likewise, in all the other studies described in this book, journal publications, reports, and conference presentations were worked on in collaboration, and sharing lead authorship, with colleagues from these various projects.

Designing a Culturally Appropriate Methodology

A culturally appropriate study on a reservation should include the opportunity for tribal participants to tell their stories. Storytelling is an important part of life and learning in Indian families. Indian peoples have historically relied on oral tradition to relay their experiences (Ambler, 1995; Montejo, 1994). This was a mixed-methods study whereby both quantitative (survey) and qualitative (interviews) data were collected. Even though among Indian peoples a qualitative approach is more compatible with traditional ways of knowing because qualitative studies examine relationships and the whole (Crazy Bull, 1997), obtaining quantitative data was not a problem. In fact, we have experienced that when stakeholders (i.e., community partners, study participants, Indians, and non-Indians) are included in preparatory discussions of the projects and their ideas considered, they also welcome explanations about the details of the study and more often than not, they do not object to some of the "scientific" impositions. For example, in some of our work, after explaining the rationale for selecting large sample sizes (i.e., issues of statistical power) or conducing an experimental design (i.e., issues of internal validity), in subsequent studies community partners have questioned our selection of a "small" sample sizes and our not using a randomized clinical trial to study the desired research questions.

More challenging was making sure measures were identified that had been "normed" for use with Indian people, which was a difficult task. In this study, survey questions were adapted so that they would more accurately portray reservation home life. Researchers who are not Indian can utilize consultants and tribal participants in adapting measures to the needs of the Indian community. We propose that as more researchers study Indians, more culturally appropriate measures will become available. Given the topics we selected for discussion in this chapter, we do not provide examples of how measures were adapted in this particular study. Individuals interested in learning more about this step are encouraged to contact the authors, who will gladly share this information.

Another cultural challenge arises when considering whom to assess. In this study, only mothers reported on their children's behaviors. From a research point of view, it would have been ideal to also obtain information from the children's teachers given that children spend a considerable amount of time in schools. Although it would be ideal to obtain reports from teachers, a culturally sensitive researcher would be aware or would learn that in this particular tribe, though not unlike many others, there was a long history of a tenuous relationship with the school district, which happens to be off the reservation. Concerns about obtaining teachers' reports stem from the significant history of ethnic animosity that exists between the reservation and the adjacent town where the children attend school and because the majority of teacher reports would be from teachers who are not Indian. Throughout the 1980s and 1990s in this region the relationship between Indians on the reservation and the non-Indian adjacent townspeople was strained as treaty rights were being contested (Grossman & McNutt, 2001). Tensions between the communities increased such that racism escalated to the point where Indians were verbally harassed and physically assaulted. Given these historical factors, insisting on obtaining teachers' reports of the children's behaviors may have isolated Indian women and affected their participation. Also, it is unclear whether the information obtained from the teachers would have been negatively biased in light of the historical context. Certainly, obtaining information from teachers about a child's behavior can significantly strengthen a research study; however, in this particular case, awareness of historical and cultural issues strongly recommended against contacting teachers. In retrospect, however, we realize that it would have been entirely appropriate to ask the mothers what they thought of asking their children's teachers to also answer questions about their children's behaviors. Given that more teachers are becoming more open to helping and being respectful of Indian children, it could have been possible that the mothers would have been open to asking teachers to assess their children. Depending on the mothers' feedback, the investigator would have then proceeded accordingly.

Another concern about relying only on mothers' reports is that the Indian women might not be willing to disclose sensitive information to a tribal member who lives off the reservation. This is an entirely valid concern that is experienced by anyone who has ever participated in a research project. But this is especially true for Indians and other racial/ethnic minority groups in this and other countries that have had a long history of racist, discriminatory, and prejudicial practices by the government or dominant culture. For example, early contact with Europeans frequently resulted in death and disempowerment (Gray, Yellow Bird, & Coates, 2008). Federal treaties, all of which were broken, enabled the government to seize land. Indian children were placed in boarding schools, many against the will of parents, to assimilate them into the dominant culture. In boarding schools they were not allowed to practice their religion, spiritual traditions, or speak their language, and they experienced physical and sexual abuse (Gray et al., 2008). Laws were passed by state and city governments against Indians; Indians could only enter a town to trade their goods and could not be present after sunset; bounties were placed on Indian scalps; and massacres were legal (United Native America, n.d.). From 1970 to 1976 between 25% and 50% of American Indian women accessing Indian Health Service were sterilized against their will (Dillingham, 1977). In this particular study, the Indian women appeared to be reassured by the nonresident researcher role because they assumed that the information provided would be kept confidential. A researcher who is not Indian may be afforded the same level of respect and confidence if respect for the cultural practices and understanding of historical contexts are taken into serious consideration, especially if he or she has spent time on the reservation.

Data Collection

Active involvement of the RA and tribal members in the collection of data can ensure that the study is accepted by tribal participants as one that can be trusted, one they would want to be involved in, and one in which they can feel comfortable answering questions without fear of reprisals. Additionally, as the RA and tribal members become active participants in conducting the study, they are acquiring research skills and can serve as future cultural brokers for other research studies on the reservation. The following procedures were followed in this study, but can be adapted for other reservations as well:

- Contact the RA to set a time to gather data that is mutually convenient; defer to the RA if he or she is an elder.
- Ask the RA to tell people about the study. A leaflet can be posted around the reservation, but word of mouth is more productive and culturally appropriate.
- First, conduct a pilot study to get input from the RA and tribal members about the design of the study.

  a. Community members ($N = 15$) filled out the survey, feedback was encouraged, questions were answered, and changes were suggested.

   b. Of these 15 tribal members, three participated in an in-depth interview to assess the appropriateness of the interview protocol.

- Make changes to the study or measures if requested. If unable to do this, explain why to the tribal members. They will understand.
- Be flexible. For example, mothers were the focus of this study, but not all Indian mothers are biological mothers of the children. It is common among Indian families to find grandparents, aunts, stepmothers, cousins, and siblings rearing the child (Dykeman & Nelson, 1995). Thus, female caretakers, who had the focal child presently residing with them, were included in this study. For these same reasons, in the longitudinal study of Chilean families (Chapter 4) and the randomized clinical trial study with African Americans (Chapter 5) described in this book, the studies enrolled caregivers and not just biological mothers.
- Arrive several days before the study commences so people see you are back on the reservation. You can work out any last-minute details with the RA or other tribal members. If possible, stay on the reservation with a family or in a reservation motel.
- Defer to your RA or elder tribal member for directions as to how to proceed in terms of accessing the space and so forth. The RA advised the researcher to ask the tribal men in person to set up tables and chairs. They were given a gift of tobacco for their help.
- Involve community members as much as possible. Indian children made a colorful poster to hang up at the research sight and were given a few dollars.
- Pay tribal members in cash for their time because it is not up to the researcher to decide how a person's money is spent. We understand academic centers often require some form of documentation (proof) that payment was made to the appropriate person, sometimes even asking for social security numbers. Some of these requirements produce concerns about IRS involvement. Later in this chapter we describe the arrangement made with the University to pay study participants without having to obtain their social security numbers.
- Take time to answer their questions, and be willing to self-disclose about yourself and why you are doing the study. The tribal members should have already met you at other tribal events. If they appear

unsure of you, however, defer to your RA or elder to re-introduce you to them.

- Schedule interviews at times and places that are convenient for the members. Be willing to provide a ride, or a babysitter, if needed.
- Be flexible with the study timeline so you can be involved in reservation life, learn more about the culture, and can change scheduled data collection times if tribal members have to attend important familial or tribal events.

Data Analysis

Once the quantitative data regarding gambling behaviors were analyzed using statistics and the qualitative data were transcribed, it became evident that the information collected in the interviews appeared to be more accurate in terms of the gambling behaviors of the women. Indian women who scored lower on the measure of problem or pathological gambling were more forthcoming in the interviews about the true extent of their gambling behaviors. This speaks to the importance of conducting studies of Indian people that include qualitative data collection methods. Based on our experiences, we believe that it is essentially a universal preference for people to be more open to telling their stories through open-ended questions than from filling out standardized questionnaires composed with closed-ended items.

The nuances of language and culture that were specific to this tribe became evident in the transcripts. It is important at this point to hire an Indian transcriber or to transcribe the interviews and then go over the transcripts with the RA or tribal elder. These individuals can highlight linguistic and cultural nuances to assure that you are getting an accurate depiction of what the tribal members were trying to convey. The same is true for the quantitative data: share and discuss the results with the RA. Also from our other research experiences, the interpretation of findings can be much richer if collaborators and study participants are included in the interpretation of the results.

Reporting Results

Results need to be presented in a format that is meaningful to tribal members. Results of this study were shared with tribal members. The researcher met with the RA, tribal chairman and tribal council members, and some participants over coffee to discuss the results. This led to an in-depth discussion of the results, their interpretations of the results, the overall impact of gambling on the reservation, as well as future research. Of note is that the written format of the study was not as important to tribal members as a face-to-face discussion of the findings. The researcher collaborated with the RA to prepare a formal dissemination of the results at conferences.

Maintaining an objective viewpoint is the standard when conducting and reporting research results. According to Hammersley and Atkinson (1996), insiders need to guard against over-rapport with the participants that they are studying. The opposing view is that there is a need to gather information about American Indians from an insider perspective based on Indian histories and perspectives because more meaningful interpretations can be obtained (Swisher, 1996).

Giving Back and Participation in Reservation Life

When conducting research on Indians, the research needs to be managed in such a way that one gives back to the Indian people. "Giving back" is a cultural value in Indian communities (Garcia, 2000) and, interestingly, it is an integral component of any type of community-based research. The American Indian author was raised to believe in the cyclical nature of life, and she was grateful that so many people on the reservation had been influential in making sure her childhood was happy. It was now her turn to give back to the community as a gesture of thanks to them. Examples of ways to give back are provided later in this chapter using as illustration some of the activities done by the researcher herself.

Research on the reservation needs to be a partnership between the researcher and Indians, and when researchers make use of participants' ideas and time, they must provide resources, skills, employment, and/or training (Davis & Reid, 1999). Additionally, inclusion of RAs in the analysis of the data and preparation of reports, manuscripts, and conference presentations serves to legitimize the results while allowing the RA(s) to experience the world of academia or research. It must be kept in mind that conducting research in this collaborative fashion results in a slower process than one might be accustomed to. From our experience, extremely fruitful collaborations and high-quality studies can be designed if one is able to suspend the concept of time and allow both the RA(s) and the Indian community to get used to the idea of research that is conducted *with* them and not *on* them.

Being an active participant in reservation life is important for a researcher. How one conducts oneself while on the reservation is critical to the success of the research study. Even though in the study described here the tribal members were paid $20 for their time, payment was not the most important aspect in determining their cooperation. It was more important that the researcher had established relationships with tribal members, helped people in need, especially elders and children, provided rides and other favors for people, and also participated in tribal activities. This participation has to be genuine and not just to complete the study. However, this is not to suggest that participants should not be properly compensated. We strongly believe that they should be properly compensated even if culturally they may be willing to participate with no compensation. Some examples of the researcher's participation in the community during the 6-week stay of this study were as follows: driving a young man to summer school every morning, fixing the plumbing at the house where she was staying, planting trees at the burial grounds, participating in long talks with elders about the past, organizing the trapping of two bears that were visiting the home where she was staying, helping people with school work, driving people shopping and to doctor appointments, camping with the children, participating in canoe races, attending the powwow, and helping to set up a fry-bread stand. All of these acts of participation take time, but they allow one the opportunity to learn more about the culture and to better assist in designing effective policies and much-needed interventions. Next, we used a study of gambling, alcohol, smoking, and drug use on the reservation as an additional example of mixed-methods research.

THE RESEARCH QUESTIONS AND THEORETICAL MODEL (STUDY 2)

Although the mixed-methods study described previously was not a comorbidity study of gambling behaviors with alcohol, smoking, and/ or drug use, the women who were interviewed noted relationships between gambling and alcohol or drug use on the reservation since the opening of the casino. These data and the concerns raised by the tribal women subsequently led to a focus group study of gambling, alcohol, smoking, and drug use on the reservation. Eight focus groups were conducted as "talking circles" (2006 and 2007) with 49 participants between the ages of 12 and 78 (Momper, Delva, & Reed, in press). This situation illustrates how the use of mixed methods in conducting research can become an evolving process wherein data collected in one stage can inform the next stage, which can inform the next stage, and so on. This is of particular importance when conducting research among understudied and diverse populations, where the "insider" point of view is barely reflected in the scant research, if at all.

This study employed focus groups as talking circles, which are a traditional method of group communication in American Indian communities. Additionally, an emergent design methodology for the focus groups was utilized in which the moderator and the RA came to the initial group with a plan and allowed the plans for subsequent groups to evolve from the input from that group (Morgan, Fellows, & Guevara, 2008). Keeping in mind that in an emergent design study the research questions evolve and change during the study (Creswell, 2003), the following research questions were initially proposed to begin the study: (1) Do American Indians who gamble at the casino report an increase in their smoking while gambling, drinking while gambling, and drug use while gambling? (2) Is there an association between frequency (how often) and levels (at risk, problem, or pathological) of gambling and an increase or decrease in alcohol or drug use? (3) Do gamblers and casino employees who are nonsmokers or former smokers report higher rates of exposure to secondhand smoke than gamblers and casino employees who are smokers?

Project Implementation

Data received from the initial explanatory study led to a subsequent focus group study of gambling, alcohol, smoking, and drug use on the reservation. When the study was initially conceptualized from the data, the author went to the reservation to discuss the possibility of continuing to conduct research with reservation participants.

Obtaining Tribal Permission/Consent

Elder tribal members who had previously worked with on the study described earlier were consulted about the proposed study and agreed that it was an important next step in gathering data with tribal members. The formerly hired RA, now referred to as a research associate, discussed the proposed study with the tribal chairman over their morning coffee. Then she instructed the author to meet with the tribal chairman in person to get the necessary letter of approval, which was later received.

Cultural Brokering or Negotiating Two Worlds

At this stage in the process an IRB application was submitted. The IRB required that the receipt for participant payments include participants' social security numbers. A discussion ensued regarding historical issues surrounding relationships between researchers and Indians and the lack of trust that occurred. Once this was discussed with the IRB staff, the participant payment receipt forms were approved without the necessary social security numbers. At this point in the study there was a recognition by the author that as the social work researcher she was the cultural broker not only for the Indians but also for the academic community. The IRB personnel were happy to assist in this process as long as she explained the reasons certain procedures were not culturally appropriate or would make it difficult to access Indian participants in the research.

Additionally, the research associate and the first two groups of elderly participants (to be discussed later on in this chapter) questioned the initial proposal's age limit and asked why children could not be included in the study. The response was that it would make the study more difficult to get approval from the University IRB. The participants' response to this was that we needed to include children and to not let those kinds of "rules" get in the way of conducting the study. When the IRB was approached with the decision to change the age range from 18 to 85 years of age to 12 to 85 years of age, it was quickly approved by the IRB. The author's preconceived notions about not including children were debunked, and the study design was approved rather quickly.

Hire Tribal Members

For this study the research assistant was rehired and promoted to research associate. The author had to justify the promotion to the University's Human Resources office because the worker did not have the necessary academic background. A written statement of her life and research experience was composed and accepted by the University, with a note discussing how important it is in Indian country to have lived experiences and be an elder. In addition, the research associate was required to fill out paperwork to become a temporary employee of the University. Even this step in the process was difficult, but fortunately the author had to make a trip to the reservation on another matter and was able to assist and describe the paperwork and the reasons why it was needed. This is a step in the research process that might need to be completed with the assistance of the researcher. The issue is not that the forms are difficult; rather, they are viewed as intrusive to Indian people. An observer from the reservation who would also act as a notetaker for the groups was hired to assist in the study as well.

Design a Culturally Appropriate Methodology

A total of eight talking circles, 1.5–2 hours in length, were conducted over the course of this study. This culturally appropriate method of conducting focus groups has been successfully used by other Indian researchers; it is familiar to Indians because they historically rely on oral tradition to relay experiences (Ambler, 1995; Becker, Affonso, & Blue Horse Beard, 2006; Hodge, Fredericks, & Rodriguez, 1996; Montejo, 1994; Strickland, 1999). Keep in mind that these were not spiritual talking circles, but the use of a talking circle format as it was familiar to all participants. The first two groups were conducted in December 2006 to introduce the elders to the group methods and to get their input on the study design; the remaining six groups were conducted in April 2007. Purposive sampling techniques were utilized with input from the research associate, the observer, and an elder female tribal member. Elders are an important resource in Indian communities; engaging elders early on assures access to other tribal members, because they look to the elders for guidance.

Data Collection

The research associate arranged with the tribal chairman and tribal administration staff a place to meet for the talking circles. At this point in the research process, the outside researcher has to be willing to forego beliefs about time, such as being "on time," and know that the groups will take place but that participants may not be punctual. Being sensitive with the population means being able to be flexible and relaxed about these activities. In fact, at a recent Indian and University meeting that the University wanted to host for tribal health leaders, the entire meeting was timed. The University moderator, who was told not to impose time constraints on Indians, continued throughout the entire meeting to impose a time schedule. It was very uncomfortable for the Indians because they had to submit to the dominant view of what "time" entails.

For her study, the researcher was fortunate to know her culture and to know that in the first group session and subsequent sessions that starting on time was not going to happen. For example, the first group session was to have taken place in a conference room and a key to the room was to be provided by a staff person prior to the session. The staff person would be present to open the door to the room, as it was after hours, and to open the front door of the building to let participants in. However, this person had a family member that was ill and did not make the session. At this point the research associate found another room that was suitable. A young person was stationed at the side entryway to let people in. The meeting did not start "on time," and not everyone came "on time." However, this situation created an opportunity for more informal communications to take place. For example, participants had time to talk to the author, the research associate, and the observer about the study and to go over the consent forms in depth. Additionally, there was time to check the recording equipment, and the research associate had time to set up the food for the participants. Participants also had time to catch up on news about family and friends. The ability to acknowledge that the groups would occur, but not in any particular time frame or in the manner conceived for the study, added to the successful completion of the project. Once everyone arrived and had an opportunity to sign the consent forms, which were explained orally and in written format, questions were encouraged and answered and the importance of the confidentiality of the information provided by other group members was discussed. Of note is that because of this flexibility about time, the earlier participants who had already signed all of the necessary forms took it upon themselves to explain the consent forms to the later participants.

People left to go outside to smoke halfway through the first group session. In subsequent sessions a smoking break was built into the schedule. Ironically, this project was in part funded by the University of Michigan Tobacco Research Network, but we had to let participants take a smoking break and also bring loose tobacco to elder participants for ceremonial use as a gift.

Unlike typical focus groups in which the moderator plays an active role in eliciting information, in talking circles the moderator tempers this by deferring to elders. Tribal participants sat in a circle around the table, everyone had an equal opportunity to speak, and elders were not interrupted and were allowed to speak for as long as they wanted. If an elder is sharing wisdom with participants, it is inappropriate for the moderator, or younger members, to interrupt. The only person who can intercede is another elder. The initial Focus Group Guide with a list of three questions was used for this session: *(1)* We are trying to understand more about how people in our tribe think about gambling. Can we talk about that? *(2)* We are trying to understand more about how people in our tribe think about smoking. Can we talk about that? *(3)* We are trying to understand more about how people in our tribe think about drinking. Can we talk about that? *(4)* We are trying to understand more about how people in our tribe think about drug use. Can we talk about that? and *(5)* If you could conduct a study of gambling, smoking, and alcohol and other drug use on the reservation, how would it look to you (composition of participants, questions to ask, and in what format—quantitative and/or qualitative)? An observer, who was a tribal member, took notes during the sessions; the observer noted nonverbal behaviors, described who was talking and what they were talking about, listed quotes, and detailed group interaction. Following this first group session, the study team debriefed so that the plans for the subsequent talking circle sessions evolved from the nonverbal behaviors, the discussions, impressions, and group interaction of the first session.

This emergent design approach to the groups is a relatively new concept in conducting focus groups. Morgan, Fellows, and Guevara (2008) define "emergence between focus groups" as a method whereby the principal investigator/moderator comes to the initial group session with a plan for how to conduct that group, while allowing the plans for conducting the later groups to evolve from the analysis and interpretations from the earlier session. The emergent design method for this study allowed the tribal elders from the first two groups to have input into the composition of the groups, the content of the questions, and the appropriate moderating style for the other six sessions. This method is particularly appropriate for Indian people because too often a historically suspicious relationship has existed between Indian people and the research community. In order to allay these fears, this study was conducted in a collaborative manner, leaving ample time for tribal members to be full participants in this research study.

Elders from the first two groups requested that children be included in the study, and that the talking circles be divided by gender and age. In emergent design this is called "segmentation" and allows different perspectives to emerge (Morgan, Fellows, & Guevara, 2008, 2006). Elders also requested that select members be invited more than once, consistent with a multi-stage approach to focus groups, which enables participants to gain comfort in speaking (Morgan, 2006). This multi-stage approach assured that all participants' input was considered because Indians do not always speak until a level of comfort is reached and that may be at the end of a group meeting (Strickland, 1999). Additionally, a female elder attended five of the talking circles because elders stated, "You still got to have an elder there—somebody with more knowledge, a guide for when younger kids come." This elder did not attend all of the sessions because a family member was ill, and she had to care for this person. This too is an important component of conducting social work research with Indians. There must be a willingness to understand and expect participants to have family and community events that they must attend to; in Indian culture, family and community take precedence over other things. Participants from one talking circle requested a circle to specifically talk about their OxyContin use; the research associate and female elder approved conducting this group without an elder present.

Before each talking circle, participants completed a brief demographic questionnaire (age, gender, marital status, educational attainment, employment status, and household income). Food was provided because this is appropriate when tribal people get together to have a "feast." The sessions were digitally audio-recorded, and all participants were paid $50 for their time and willingness to share with the other group members.

Data Analysis

The data collected in this study consisted of verbatim transcripts as well as observer and debriefing notes. The author contracted out the digital recordings for transcribing, but she later found that some of the nuances of the dialect and culture were not interpreted accurately because the transcriber was not Indian and was not familiar with the culture. For example, the transcriber was not familiar with the concept of the "Creator," the spiritual term for what other people might call "God." Additionally, the transcriber appeared to transcribe negatively words she could not understand, so that the context of the transcription changed from a positive to a negative view of Indians. The author then proceeded to re-transcribe all of the transcripts so that accurate data were received. This experience taught the researcher the importance of having someone familiar with the dialect and culture complete this step in the research process. All of the talking circle transcripts were analyzed using content analysis procedures to identify important phrases, patterns, and themes (Krippendorff, 2004). A theme is a pattern in the data that describes and organizes concepts (Boyatzis, 1998). First, transcripts were read by the author of this chapter and a second American Indian reader, a doctoral student, to get an overall understanding of the content of the discussions and compare observer and debriefing notes to ensure that nothing was missed. Second, each author independently coded the transcripts manually, highlighting the most important aspects of the information shared by the participants. Manual coding involves highlighting text segments and then applying codes in the margins (Drisko, 2004). After concurring with each other, data were then entered into NVivo software designed to code text with a user-created code list that notes the frequency and placement of each code (Richards, 1999). Third, we met to concur on the central themes that emerged from both the manual and NVivo coding of the transcripts. Further discussions occurred, and the author and the reader agreed on the overarching themes of the groups.

Reporting Results

Data from this study have been shared with tribal staff who worked on the project as well as other key tribal people. At this time a decision was made to share some of the information, without identifying participants, that was pertinent to the social services staff on the reservation, such as prevalence and perceptions of drug use. This information could be utilized to write grant proposals to obtain funding to conduct interventions. The key to reporting the results of a study with Indian people is to do so in a timely manner so that the information can assist social workers and other helping professionals to either collect additional clarifying information or apply for funding for prevention, intervention, and treatment programs that might be needed.

CONCLUSION

Informed by this work, several additional mixed-methods studies are under development on the reservation with the full support of the community. As of this writing, funding is being sought to conduct these studies. One of these mixed-methods studies involves a combination of stratified and cluster sampling (sampling and analytic issues related to these techniques are described in Chapter 3) of several hundred Indian families in order to inform the development of a randomized clinical trial (a topic discussed in Chapter 5).

The use of both methods, quantitative and qualitative, to better understand the Indian way of life is certainly appropriate because too often Indians have filled out surveys that were foreign to them. In revising standardized instruments accordingly and adding the qualitative/oral piece to any study of Indians, we are allowing Indian peoples to respond in a way that comes more naturally. From the studies that the author has conducted and the contacts she has made as a social work researcher, she has learned that Indian peoples are not against research despite the general perception that they are not willing to participate in research. The concern is more about the way research has been traditionally conducted *on* them as opposed to *with* them.

In summary, this chapter was written as a guide to assist researchers conducting mixed-methods research in a culturally sensitive manner by describing how two studies were conducted with Indian people on a reservation. Bridging the gap between the dominant culture and Indian culture is a journey that will enrich all involved in the process as well as society at large.

3

Conducting Large-Scale Population-Based Survey Research

Worldwide, and in the United States in particular, numerous population-based surveys are conducted to examine the extent to which a particular behavior, problem, belief, attitude, or perception exists, to describe how these are distributed across characteristics of the population (gender, age groups, etc.), and to understand how these are associated with other behaviors, problems, belief, attitudes, and perceptions. The importance of these studies lies in their ability to identify the extent to which a particular problem exists and how it differs among various groups of people who may be exposed to different factors or to the same factors differentially (Kish, 1965).

Surveys with large representative samples are needed in order to generalize the findings to the general population. Some of the most well-known population surveys in the United States are the National Health and Nutrition Examination Survey (NHANES) (http://www.cdc.gov/nchs/nhanes.htm) and the Youth Risk Behavior Surveillance System (http://www.cdc.gov/HealthyYouth/yrbs/index.htm), which are funded by the Centers for Disease Control and Prevention. Other large studies include the Monitoring the Future (MTF) (http://www.monitoring-thefuture.org) and the National Survey of Drug Use and Health (NSDUH) (http://www.oas.samhsa.gov/NSDUHlatest.htm), which are both funded by the National Institute on Drug Abuse; and the Collaborative Psychiatric Epidemiology Surveys (CPES) (http://www.icpsr.umich.edu/CPES), which is funded by the National Institute on Mental Health. These are just a few examples of the large number of such surveys in the United States. In this chapter we illustrate the conduct of population-based studies by using as an example the implementation of a large school-based survey of substance use in several Latin American countries. The countries are Costa Rica, Dominican Republic, El Salvador, Guatemala, Honduras, Panama, and Nicaragua. The project's methodology followed an etic approach. Its main purpose was not to identify culturally specific information between and within each country but to obtain detailed information about drug use patterns among school-attending youth. This information was used to inform the corresponding governments of where some of their prevention resources should be focused when they involved the school-attending population. Despite using an etic approach, the instrument and survey approach were pilot tested in each country, and the instrument was translated, back translated, and harmonized using input from the collaborators and other individuals (i.e., school teachers, school counselors) from each of the countries. More than a year was spent on these tasks.

Notwithstanding the fact that the purpose of this project was not to study the epidemiology of drug use via a cross-cultural lens, we nonetheless discuss it in this book because its implementation involved a number of activities that required collaborators to navigate different cultural and geopolitical situations, some of them of a very sensitive nature (Delva & Castillo, in press). Through these examples, we hope readers will acquire a better understanding of the inner workings of these complicated multi-national projects. Specifically, we describe what guided the formulation of the research question(s), the theoretical model, and the development and implementation of the project. In addition, as we mentioned in Chapter 1 and presented in Chapter 2, we discuss at least two facets of the study that we think are particularly important to highlight. First, we highlight the importance of building partnerships between country researchers and international organizations, and this includes a discussion of protection issues for human subjects. Second, we describe power analyses and the analytic strategy of accounting for clustering when conducting the statistical analyses. We believe these two points will be helpful to researchers planning their survey research studies.

THE RESEARCH QUESTIONS AND THEORETICAL MODEL

Until the 1990s and even until the early twenty-first century, information about substance use in Latin America relied primarily on data obtained from hospitalization mentions, treatment centers, and police and traffic accident reports (Caris, 1992). It is critical to study hospitalization patterns, treatment service utilization, and crime statistics among individuals who consume alcohol because of the burden of disease that befalls people who experience these problems and the economic and social impact on the general population. These individuals, however, are not representative of the general population. In other words, most people who drink alcohol do not consume in ways that people who meet diagnostic criteria for alcoholism do. Furthermore, these data were not systematically collected from all the hospitals, treatment centers, and police reports or through proper sampling strategies; they relied on convenience samples. Thus, to better inform their national policy on substance use the Organization of American States Inter-American Drug Abuse Control Commission (OAS-CICAD in Spanish) devised several initiatives to fill this gap in knowledge. One of these initiatives was the creation of the multilateral evaluation mechanism (MEM) in 1999 " . . . with the objective of increasing coordination, dialogue, and cooperation within the 34 [Organization of American States] member states in order to confront the drug problem more efficiently" (http://www.cicad.oas.org/MEM/ENG/About.asp). A second initiative, one that involved U.S. researchers, was the submission of a competitive grant proposal to the National Institute on Drug Abuse (NIDA). It is this second effort that we describe in this chapter. This project was led by Dr. James Anthony, who then was at the Johns Hopkins University, and it included collaboration with the OAS-CICAD and the investigators from seven countries. This study was the first-ever multi-country survey of substance use among school-attending youth in Latin America

(Dormitzer et al., 2004). At the time, one of the authors of this book (Delva) was the project manager and was responsible for its day-to-day operation.

The theoretical model that guided the work was a risk and protective factors approach in order to identify those factors that could lead to an increased likelihood of youth using substances (risk factors) and those that could serve to buffer or protect youth from using substances (protective factors). It also allowed for the investigation of the way(s) by which risk and protective factors, uniquely and in combination, would be associated with differences in substance use initiation and consumption patterns (Hawkins, Catalano, & Miller, 1992; Newcomb, Maddahian, & Bentler, 1986; Werner & Smith, 2001). In addition, the formulation of the research questions was guided by four basic rubrics of epidemiology as espoused by Anthony (Anthony, 2002; Anthony & VanEtten, 1998). These four rubrics consist of addressing questions about the prevalence and incidence of substance use, how these vary between individuals (e.g., distributed across demographic characteristics), understanding etiological underpinnings, and identifying the potential mechanisms by which youth initiate substance use and progress to more deleterious use. We next describe what we believe are key aspects of the development and implementation of the project.

PROJECT IMPLEMENTATION

By the time NIDA funded this project, a number of activities had taken place over the prior decade that set the stage for this project to be funded. As part of its mandate to address drug trafficking and drug consumption issues, the OAS-CICAD had been planning to develop a more systematic data-collection mechanism for Latin American countries to use on an ongoing basis in order to obtain more valid, reliable, and timely data about substance use. As a result of the network of individuals with interest and experience in or with substance use research that developed over this period of time, the idea of conducting school surveys of drug use came to mind. While this idea was under development, these investigators were engaged in different types of collaborations through program evaluation projects, analyses of secondary data, and writing of manuscripts. Some of the investigators had, in prior years, attended

Johns Hopkins University to extend their education and as such were able to establish closer links with researchers in the United States. By the time the project was funded, at least a decade of planning and collaboration had taken place among the individuals.

It is important to highlight that this project could not have been done without the professional and personal relationships that had been built over time. Getting a large multi-country project funded was the result of good science and of a tightly developed network of collaborators. It is unlikely that a project of this magnitude would have been successful without the time these investigators spent working together. In a true sense, establishment of these long-term relationships is a process that requires substantial investment and it is one that closely mirrors the activities described in Chapter 2, where the emphasis was on building mutually beneficial collaborations with American Indian communities. These types of long-term relationships, though among different individuals and organizations, were also absolutely necessary to conduct the longitudinal study of drug use in Santiago, Chile, described in Chapter 4.

Human Subjects Protection

Because this project was funded by NIDA, a U.S. organization, U.S. human subjects regulations had to be applied to the participating countries. This meant that not only the U.S. Institutional Review Board (IRB) but also the corresponding countries' IRBs had to review and approve the project. This was a good idea because it would allow for local application of human subjects protection criteria and standards. However, each country's IRB was supposed to follow U.S. operating procedures. One of these procedures included making sure the IRB membership was diverse, that it included males and females, researchers and nonresearchers, and community representatives. Countries needed to set up an IRB if they did not have one, and the membership of these IRBs and operating procedures (how proposals are reviewed and voted upon) had to follow U.S. standards. These regulations received three types of responses. Most researchers welcomed this imposition. These investigators indicated that they perceived this situation as an opportunity for their institution's human subjects procedures to improve as a result of these additional criteria. In countries without IRBs, researchers looked forward to the opportunity to create such a body so that their countries could pay more attention to human subjects protection issues in light of their history (very recent at the time) of human rights violations. On the other hand, two researchers met the news with considerable disdain. They saw this situation as yet another example of the United States meddling in their domestic affairs—a very appropriate concern. Only after extensive discussions about this process among all investigators and the realistic concern that funding for a particular country may not come through if local IRB approval could not be obtained did these investigators agree to follow U.S. procedures. In the end, only one of the 10 co-investigators continued to have some reservations about the project, but with the assistance of his peers, he came through and led the project in his country quite well. A lot of meals were consumed and substantial socialization took place to accomplish this task successfully. Finally, a third category of investigators' responses consisted of those who were indifferent about these impositions. Essentially, these individuals were not bothered one way or another with the "extra" IRB requirements. They saw it as another part of research that needed to be attended to.

Implementing the project also involved countless hours of coordination of which ongoing communication was a key component. Substantial communication occurred via e-mail, extensive traveling by the U.S. investigators to the other participating countries, some traveling of the country investigators to the United States (this was more expensive to accomplish and was done with less frequency), and some communication by phone and fax. Anyone who has worked in developing countries understands the logistical and financial constraints of making international calls. More often than not, phone lines are not set up for long distance calls and special approval is needed to use those few selected phones that are available for international calls. If an issue needed immediate attention, the investigator could not simply pick up the phone and call. Hence, we often relied on e-mail or on investigators using their own phones (and personal funds) to make international calls. Nowadays, international work has become considerably easier to accomplish with the advent of Internet-based communication programs such as SKYPE (http://www.skype.com), that allow for free international communication to take place via conference calls and even with video cameras. In fact, this is a main tool of communication utilized in the longitudinal project in Santiago, Chile, described in the next chapter.

Having described in some detail the research questions and theoretical model that guided this particular study, and having provided examples of certain implementation activities, we now move to a discussion of the two key research components of the project. These include a detailed description of some important aspects of the power analyses necessary for these types of studies and an overview of statistical approaches for these types of research designs and data. Some aspects of the project that are not described in this chapter, such as questionnaire construction, administration, training of personnel, and data entering and checking, among others, are described in other sections. For this particular population-based cross-sectional survey, we thought it was important to highlight power and statistical analyses for clustered data because it has been our experience that most social work researchers and many researchers in other disciplines who have not been exposed to survey research are not aware of critical survey research details.

POWER ANALYSIS AND STATISTICAL CONSIDERATION WHEN ANALYZING CLUSTERED DATA

Information on the power analyses conducted might be of value to individuals seeking to conduct similar studies. (Note that for more complex power analysis estimations, such as the one presented here, it is always important to collaborate with a statistician who has expertise in conducting power analysis for the design planned.) This section does not include a discussion about cross-cultural elements because these were not considered in the design of this multi-country project. However, we do discuss issues that impact some population groups (i.e., minorities) that should be taken into consideration in subsequent studies.

It is well-known that power analyses require information on the study's *(a)* sample size, *(b)* effect size or magnitude of the association, *(c)* alpha level (or desired probability of committing a Type I error—the probability of incorrectly rejecting the null hypothesis or, in other words, to incorrectly find a statistically significant finding when it should not have been significant), *(d)* beta level (or desired probability of committing a Type II error—the probability of incorrectly failing to reject the null hypothesis or, in other words, that an observable difference exists but it is not detected, and *(e)* the projected analyses (Cohen, 1988). Additional considerations in power analysis include taking into account *(f)* the type of design (longitudinal, cross-sectional) and *(g)* whether the data are nested (clustering) (Cochran, 1977; Kish, 1965). In the study conducted in Latin America, criteria a–f were taken into account. At that time, criterion g was not taken into account in the sample size calculations because insufficient information existed on the extent of clustering to allow for an a priori correction. However, in this chapter we provide an illustration of one of several ways to look at the extent of clustering to better inform the researcher's sample selection.

For the type of study conducted using a cross-sectional design, one that consisted of testing numerous research questions that involved predicting or explaining dichotomous dependent variables (whether students consumed a substance in their lifetime, in the past year, or in the prior 30 days), power analyses needed to incorporate the information listed above under f plus an additional step: consideration of the odds of exposure. This is needed because of the dichotomous nature of the variables. Table 3.1 illustrates this. Some of the data in these tables are

Table 3.1 Magnitude of an Association (Odds Ratio) Between a Dependent Variable (Marijuana Use in the Past Year) and a Risk Factor (Having Friends Who Also Smoke Marijuana) That Can Be Significantly Detected Assuming a Sample Size of 2400 Participants

	Drug Use Prevalence			
Exposure Odds for Risk Factor	1	10	25	50
50:50	3.3	1.4	1.3	1.3
30:70	3.1	1.5	1.3	1.3
5:95	5.0	2.0	1.7	1.6

Note: The cells are odds ratios that can be detected as statistically significant at conventional levels of 0.05 with 80% power for various levels of marijuana prevalences and exposure odds to the risk factor among non-marijuana users (non-cases in epidemiological language). Nowadays, numerous software programs exist that allow the estimation of sample size curves according to different specifications, such as the ones described earlier. The above analyses assume a sample size of 2400 individuals. Larger sample sizes would yield more power; smaller samples sizes, less power. We find creating tables such as the one above and plotting sample size curves based on various specifications to be very useful not only in helping us determine our sample sizes but also to see the particular sample size where spending additional resources to recruit study participants would be inefficient. For the sake of information, we note that a Web search for power analyses yields a number of user-friendly power analysis programs that the reader may be interested in learning to use.

taken from the proposal that was submitted to NIDA to request funding for the Latin America study and from another proposal that one of the authors (Delva) submitted to NIDA to conduct a study in Central America.

As shown in Table 3.1, if one were to assume that in the population to be studied, 1% of youth smokes marijuana and that the odds are 50:50 that a nonsmoking youth is exposed to friends who smoke and to friends who do not smoke, then odds ratios of 3.3 or higher would be considered statistically significant at a conventional level of 0.05. In other words, if 1% of the population smokes marijuana and the odds of a nonsmoking youth being exposed to friends who smoke and do not smoke are more or less equal, then magnitudes of associations (odds ratios) between the risk factor (exposure to friends who smoke) and the dependent variable (smoking marijuana) of 3.3 or higher will be detected as statistically significant at the conventional alpha level of 0.05 with 80% power.

Table 3.1 also shows that as the odds of exposure by non-cases (nonsmokers) to the risk factor decrease, larger magnitudes of associations (odds ratios) are needed for these associations to be considered statistically significant at an alpha of 0.05 with 80% power. On the other hand, with increasing prevalences, lower odds ratios can be detected as statistically significant under the same specifications. For example, if the percent of youth who smoke marijuana is 50% and the exposure odds ratio is still 50:50, then an odds ratio of 1.3 or higher will be detected as statistically significant under the same specifications.

These data are consistent with the notion that the more common an event and the more common its potential risk or protective factor, the easier the phenomenon is to detect. Conversely, associations among rarer events are more difficult to detect. These data also indicate that once the prevalence of a behavior reaches around 20%–25%, the magnitude of associations that can be detected as statistically significant are no longer different from those of behaviors with higher prevalences. These data highlight the importance that when conducting survey research with the purpose of generalizing findings to an entire population, very large samples are needed. Hence, in these types of studies, it is not uncommon for racial and ethnic minorities and other disadvantaged populations (those of lower socioeconomic status, youth in gangs, and so forth) to have lower participation rates and to be missed altogether unless a specific effort is made to oversample them. In this particular study it was cost prohibitive to design a multi-country project that would be able to oversample these other populations. When this study was designed all collaborators understood this situation. As much as they would have liked to design a study that could have ensured a more adequate representation of their corresponding minority and cultural groups and more disadvantaged populations, the study was considered appropriate given the countries' needs for reliable and trustworthy information to better inform national policy. It was understood that subsequent studies would need to be designed to capture drug use patterns among underrepresented populations in their respective countries. Also, although the measures were translated and back-translated and modifications were made to allow some flexibility in the wording of questions while harmonizing them to allow for between-country comparisons, questions that could specifically assess a unique cultural element in each country were not included. For studies that take on an etic approach, such as the present study, one can use a posteriori strategies to investigate if the country populations differ in the way they respond to the survey questions, pointing to potential cultural differences if different patterns surface. Some of this work may be conducted with item-response theory and confirmatory factor analyses to test, for example, how the students' responses to the questions vary between countries and other characteristics (Reise, Widaman, & Pugh, 1993) followed by qualitative projects that serve to provide insight about these similarities and differences. Readers who would like to read more about methodological issues researchers face when conducting population-based survey research with diverse cultures, countries, and populations are encouraged to read the book *Cross-Cultural Survey Methods*, edited by Harkness, Van de Vijver, and Mohler (2003).

Before concluding this section, we want to remind readers that if one needs a sample of 2400 individuals (the hypothetical sample size presented in Table 3.1), and it is estimated that participation rate will be 80% and that 95% of the participants will complete the questionnaires properly (5% may need to be discarded), then one would want to sample slightly more than 3000 youth ($n = 3158$). That is, to obtain an *actual* sample size of 2400 youth, divide this desired sample by the corresponding percents (0.8 and 0.95) to obtain a sample of 3158. In other words, if 3158 youth are reached, 20% will decline participation, and of those who participate 5% will provide "bad" data. So if 2400 is an optimal sample size, over 3000 youth will need to be recruited. This is a handy formula that allows researchers to obtain a quick estimate of the resources needed by taking into account information loss at various levels of the project (e.g., percent contacted out of a population list, percent that met criteria for participation out of those contacted, percent that participated out of those who met criteria, percent who appropriately completed the questionnaire out of those who participated, and so forth).

Readers can now see the extremely large samples of youth that would be needed to ensure adequate representation of cultural minorities, disadvantaged groups, and populations living in remote areas. In the United States, the budgets for the national representative studies listed earlier are out of the question in developing countries, even though the cost of conducting these surveys in developing countries is much lower. With the assistance of the Organization of American States, some countries are able to alternate conducting household surveys versus school surveys, sampling some regions consistently, and in some cases focusing on less-studied areas. Of course, there are many other methods of studying specific population behaviors such as through market and street-intercept surveys, ethnographic studies, analyses of census data, and so forth. What we have discussed in this chapter are the advantages and disadvantages of conducting large cross-sectional surveys with the purpose of generating data that can be generalized to an entire population.

Clustering of Data

Another helpful consideration in conducting power analyses is to take into account the degree of clustering that may exist in one sample because this will impact one's ability to detect statistically significant differences. By "clustering" we mean the extent to which participants' responses are not completely independent of one another because of a shared background or context. For example, kids in the same school may answer questions about drug use more similarly than kids from another school because they all belong to the same school and share a social context. Some of the responses from children in the same school may indeed depend on the fact that these children share a common space and potentially more common backgrounds than children in other schools.

In this study, the degree of drug use clustering varied between countries (Dormitzer et al., 2004). This potentially means that there are between-country differences in the extent (and perhaps rate) to which there is a "contagious" effect among drug using youth. What is it about these countries that clustering varies? Should different prevention strategies be designed as a function of differences in how youth may influence one another in these countries? Research is underway to attempt to understand the nature of these between-country, and potentially within-country, differences in drug use clustering.

In a cluster, the units that belong to the same cluster are potentially more similar to each other than to those in another cluster. As a result of this potential lack of independence, or dependency, a sample size drawn from a cluster (e.g., 10 children from 10 schools for a total of 100 children) is not the same as a same sample size of 100 randomly selected children from a population list and not from within schools. Clustered sampling, due to the dependency or homogeneity "tends to increase the variance of the sample" (Kish, 1965, p. 161), which can have an important effect in the calculation of confidence intervals and in turn results of inferential analyses. It turns out that the ratio of the variance of an estimated coefficient under a cluster design to the variance of the same estimated coefficient in a simple random sampling, of the same n, is called design effect (deff): $Deff = Variance_{(clust)}/Variance_{(srs)}$ (Cochran, 1977; Kish, 1965). In lay terms, the design effect is the effect of the type of design on the estimation of the variance as compared to what the variance would be under a random sample, generally the "gold standard" in survey research. When conducting analyses of clustered data or of data that were drawn through a combination of sampling strategies (clustered, stratified, proportional to size, and so forth), the design effect tends to be different from 1.0 because it differs from that drawn using a simple random sample, and hence needs to be corrected in the statistical analyses.

Two more concepts need to be introduced before concluding the discussion of power under clustered sampling. These are the intra-cluster correlation coefficient (ICC) and the effective sample size (ESS). The ICC is a measure of the degree to which clustering (i.e., in schools) accounts for variation in a variable of interest (i.e., drug use). It compares the between-group variance with the total variance. The ESS refers to what the sample size of a study would actually be had a random sample been drawn. With the STATA 10 data analysis and statistical

ESS = kn / {1 + [(n − 1) ICC]},

where k = number of clusters;
n = # of individuals in each cluster;
kn = actual sample size if the sampled unit is the individual;
ICC = intraclass correlation coefficient.
1 + [(n − 1) ICC = design effect

Figure 3.1 Formula to estimate effective sample size.

software program (Stata Corporation, 2008), the commands "loneway" and "xtreg, sa" allow for an easy estimation of a study's ICC. The procedure to determine effective sample size (ESS) from the expected sample size is based on the intra-class or intra-cluster correlation coefficient (ICC). The formula for the ESS is shown in Figure 3.1.

Calculation of the ESS provides the researcher with information on how much the actual sample size must be adjusted to account for dependency in the data (Donner et al., 1981). The denominator in this formula is the design effect. As the formula indicates, the larger the ICC, the larger the design effect and the smaller the ESS.

In the substance abuse field, the ICC tends to be small and range from 0.01 to 0.07 (Delva, Bobashev, & Anthony, 2000; Delva, Spencer, & Lin, 2000; Delva et al., 2006). The small amount of clustering has one important implication: that the "effect" neighborhoods may have on individual drug use may not be as large as one might imagine. This is not to say that the characteristics of one's neighborhood do not play an important role in our lives. Building healthy neighborhoods and creating healthy living spaces should certainly be among society's main goals. However, more research is needed to understand not only how neighborhoods impact individuals but also to understand the potentially reciprocal relationships between neighborhood characteristics and drug involvement, including studying mediating and moderating effects with individual characteristics.

As shown in Table 3.2, the sample size of 3000 youth, where 100 youth were sampled from 30 clusters (i.e., schools), is equivalent to the situation where 1508 or 606 youth had been randomly selected from the population, assuming an ICC of 0.01 and 0.05, respectively. Also, if clustering exists, increasing the sample size in each cluster (in this example from 100 to 200 individuals) does not really serve to increase

Table 3.2 A Hypothetical Example of Effective Sample Sizes Under
Different Conditions

			ESS	
No. of Participants per Cluster	No. of Clusters	Total No. of Participants	ICC = 0.01	ICC = 0.05
100	30	3000	1508	606
	50	5000	2513	1010
200	30	6000	2007	548
	50	10,000	3344	913

the ESS by much. To obtain a larger ESS when cluster sampling is used, it is better to increase the number of clusters than to increase the number of participants. This occurs because increasing the number of participants in each cluster does not translate into a meaningful gain of information because of the dependency or homogeneity of observations.

In the end, if there is a high degree of clustering, drawing a sample of 100 youth from 30 schools is less efficient than sampling fewer individuals (i.e., 20 or 30) from a larger number of clusters. Furthermore, if clustering exists and one ignores it in the analyses, then one is incorrectly analyzing data and potentially misestimating the statistical significance of one's results. Statistically significant findings from an analysis that ignores clustering may not be valid because the analysis did not account for the clustering of observations within social contexts. Analyses of non-random sample data are reviewed next.

Analyses of Weighted and Clustered Data

In all population studies, it is a common practice to generate weights to generalize more precisely the findings from the sample obtained to the general population from where the sample was drawn. These weights serve as "correction" factors for such situations as the occurrence of differential probabilities of selections due to the non-random sample or to combinations of random sample with other sampling strategies (e.g., stratified, clustered), oversampling of certain populations (e.g., youth, racial/ethnic minorities), and differential non-response rates, among others. If weights are properly created, the results (e.g., prevalence estimates, associations examined) are more likely to be valid.

A general rule of thumb is that weights reflect the inverse of their probability of selection. For example, if a particular population consists of 500 individuals and 20 are randomly selected, then the probability of selection of each individual is 20/500 or 0.04. The inverse of this (1/0.04) is 25. Thus, each person would receive a weight of 25, meaning that each person represents 25 other individuals not sampled for a total of 500 (20 persons 25). These weights can be transformed so that the sum of the weighted cases equals the sample size. Transforming weights in this manner is often preferred when conducting analyses because cell sizes reflect the sample "ns" as opposed to the estimated population "Ns."

Because it is likely that the researcher may be interested in over-sampling individuals with certain characteristics (i.e., immigrants, males, those of lower SES), and there is reason to believe that not everyone may be successfully contacted and that of those contacted that there will not be 100% participation, the final weight created will be based on a combination of these "rates." This results in some individuals having the same weight but others having very different weights to "correct" for their differential rates of selection and participation in the study. Many studies provide detailed information about how their weights are created.

In the Latin American study described in this chapter, weights were created taking into account the number of youth in the cities from where they were sampled and their participation rates. Most statistical software programs easily allow for the incorporation of weights. Manuals for these programs provide extensive information on how the weights are utilized in the analyses.

In the same way weights are used as corrective factors for the individual's differential probability of selection, analyses of data that were sampled using a combination of sampling strategies, often referred to as "complex sampling" (i.e., random, cluster, and stratified sampling), also need to be "corrected" for the fact that the sample is not based on a simple random sample. When participants are selected using a "complex sampling design," standard errors are no longer based on a random sampling distribution, the default in most statistical packages. The most commonly used statistical programs such as STATA by Stata Corporation (http://www.stata.com/), SAS by the SAS Institute Inc. (http://www.sas.com/), SUDAAN by RTI International (http://www.rti.org/SUDAAN/), and now SPSS by SPSS Inc. (http://www.spss.com/), among others, allow the analyses to take into account the design effects due to the complex sampling designs; however, the user needs to know the specific commands for these analyses.

Increasingly, more universities around the country are offering courses on sampling. The University of Michigan Institute for Social Research (ISR) (http://www.isr.umich.edu/home/) offers what may be the most comprehensive program on survey research and on the topics presented in this chapter. Readers interested in conducting survey research are encouraged to learn about these topics in greater detail from the ISR website and from other organizations and institutions that also provide considerable training on these analytic methods.

CONCLUSION

As we show in this chapter, it was important for the countries and the Organization of American States to conduct a multi-country study that would provide reliable data that could be generalized to their school-attending youth. This study was conducted using primarily an etic approach with some minor deviations in the questionnaire items and sampling in response to a particular country's situation. In retrospect, we realize that greater emphasis could have been paid to studying more country-specific cultural elements, but given the needs of the countries, the budget, and the state of knowledge at the time, this study was the right one, and it was what the countries wanted to do.

In this chapter we highlighted several aspects of the development and implementation of the research and some methodological considerations. As far as research implementation, the main lesson we would like our readers to appreciate is the importance of the long-term relationships, bonds, and trust that formed between the investigators—connections that, started decades earlier with smaller projects and training activities. Sensitivity was not unidirectional, as in only U.S. investigators being sensitive to the cultural backgrounds of their international partners. Rather, it was multi-directional, with all individuals working on being sensitive to all the cultures represented at the table. For example, U.S. investigators understood that in some countries the "process" could not be rushed, while researchers from these countries were very sensitive and concerned about the time constraints under which the project was operating.

Gaining "entrance" to these countries and schools was the result of decades of collaborations. It is also important to highlight that all of the countries' collaborators were involved in the design and implementation of the study. Maintaining ongoing communication was easier in some countries than others due to differences in access to technology, ability to pay, and the collaborators own ability to spend time on this project—something that could often fluctuate based on their bosses' (Minister of Health, the President's office itself) predilections. Again, these challenges were met with patience, understanding of the countries' sociopolitical and geopolitical circumstances, and support from one another in the form of resources and empathy.

As far as methodological considerations, the reader may wonder what power analyses and analyses of weighted and clustered data have to do with cross-cultural research. The answer is that they have absolutely nothing to do with each other, and at the same time they have everything to do with each other. Properly attending to the clustering and weighting of data is entirely pertinent because if one seeks to answer the following questions: To what extent does a problems occur? How is the problem distributed across the population? What factors may be associated with it? How do these associations vary as a function of contextual factors (i.e., organizational, school, city, country characteristics)?, then one needs to be extremely careful on how a sample is drawn and how the data are analyzed. Not paying the proper attention to these factors will not only limit a study's generalizability but also increase the chances of obtaining invalid findings. This could lead researchers to make incorrect policy recommendations or inappropriately recommend that certain prevention and intervention programs be supported, and others eliminated, among other serious consequences. Unfortunately, a challenge of survey research, as a result of the need for large sample sizes, is the inclusion of sufficiently large umbers of minorities or disadvantaged populations. Our experience informs us that proper inclusion is entirely possible but that this requires "enlightened" researchers, that is, researchers who understand the need to do this and who will push for this to happen, as well as political will because it means that additional resources must be added or resources redirected for this to happen despite opposition from potentially more dominant forces who do not value focusing research on specific populations.

To obtain valid findings to make better policy recommendations, the proper application of research methods (properly drawn samples) and analytical strategies (correctly weighting and analyzing complex survey data) are essential steps when conducting any research. Over the years we have learned that individuals without scientific training actually appreciate "all this fancy statistical stuff," as one individual once said, if this is communicated in an informal and easy-to-understand manner for the purpose of bridging worlds, rather than creating or enforcing hierarchical distances, between academics and the public, for instance. Interestingly, the lack of proper communication between the scientific community and the public at large has been a matter of discussion among members of the American Association for the Advancement of Science. It has been our experience that community members who understand the importance of scientific concepts begin to request that stringent scientific criteria be applied when designing studies.

We posit that the science of survey research is the same no matter where the survey is conducted. What differs is how the researcher engages with stakeholders and goes about collaborating with his or her partners of different cultural backgrounds—a theme to which we devoted extensive attention in Chapter 2 and throughout this chapter. This particular multi-country study was successful because of the long-term relationship that existed between the study's principal investigator in the United States, , the country collaborators, and the OAS-CICAD. The relationship was built on trust and mutual collaboration over many years. Similarly, the success of the study was predicated on the quality of the relationship between each of the countries' collaborators and their corresponding stakeholders that included governmental agencies (i.e., Ministries of Health, Education, Welfare, and Defense, among others), school personnel, students, and parents. The study collaborators relied on their relationships with these stakeholders to successfully implement the study in their respective countries.

4

Conducting Longitudinal Studies

Longitudinal studies, that is, studies that follow a cohort of people over time are very powerful research designs that can contribute to our understanding of the temporal association among variables of interest. In this chapter we use two examples of longitudinal studies. Both studies utilize an etic–emic approach and both are underway in urban, cosmopolitan areas. In both studies the etic approach stems from the use of standardized, previously validated instruments and a design that called for a specific research protocol. In the description of the projects we describe how the emic perspective was incorporated into the respective projects. Interestingly, we note that for both projects being culturally sensitive to the populations had less to do with cultural elements and more to do with gender and language issues and socioeconomic conditions. Hence, in this chapter when we describe activities or steps taken to be responsive to the needs of the study participants, we describe how we went about being sensitive to the individuals, families, and communities without adding the word *cultural* because we believe the issues we encountered were less about culture and more about other identities. Regardless of the labels we use, the success of these studies depended on being sensitive to the people we wanted to work with, which meant that the driving concerns were about language, gender, age, race and ethnicity, and poverty. To make it more interesting for the reader, where appropriate, we also provide results of preliminary findings that either may support or run counter to our hypotheses.

The first study we describe is the implementation of a large longitudinal project of substance use and mental health among youth and their families that is presently underway in Santiago, Chile. The project is called the Santiago Longitudinal Study (SLS), and it is funded by the National Institute on Drug Abuse. For this study, as we did in the earlier chapters, we describe what guided the formulation of the research question(s), we explain which theoretical model was chosen, and we provide examples of the development and implementation of the project. In addition to these three topics, we highlight three critical aspects of the project that we believe readers may find useful in planning their own projects. First, we emphasize the multi- and interdisciplinary collaboration that is in place. Second, we describe in detail the steps that were taken to create a questionnaire for use in a different country and culture—a questionnaire that was pilot tested and revised according to the staff and study participants' extensive feedback. Third, we present an overview of various analytical approaches that will be conducted once sufficient data are collected.

The second study consists of a longitudinal study of posttraumatic stress disorder (PTSD). This study seeks to understand PTSD as a function of the interplay of ecological and individual factors among African American adults living in the City of Detroit. This study is also underway. The study is funded by the National Institute on Drug Abuse and the National Institute on Mental Health, and it is called the Detroit Neighborhood Health Study (DNHS). From this study we present examples regarding the conceptualization of a large population-based multi-level study and the use of biomarkers to assess immunodeficiency to examine how this might be associated with traumatic event experiences and PTSD itself. We also emphasize the inter- and multi-disciplinary partnerships that exist in this project and the issues that are of a sensitive nature to these communities. Both the SLS and DNHS would not be possible without the collaboration of individuals from different disciplines.

THE SANTIAGO LONGITUDINAL STUDY

Research Questions and Theoretical Model

The prevalence of substance use is disproportionately high among Hispanic youth in the United States (Delva et al., 2005; Johnston, O'Malley, Bachman, & Schulenberg, 2008), and substance use is increasing in Latin America (United Nations Office on Drugs and Crime and the Inter-American Drug Abuse Control Commission, 2006). Yet substance use in Hispanic populations is vastly understudied. The relatively few studies with Hispanics consist mainly of cross-sectional samples or very short longitudinal designs (e.g., 2–3 years). They tend to rely on samples of school-attending youth and do not include information on biological insults that might impact later substance use. The SLS addresses many of these limitations. It builds on an extraordinary sample of 1000 young Chilean adolescents, and their families, who have been followed longitudinally since infancy. This sample was originally enrolled in conjunction with a National Institutes of Health (NIH)–supported study of the behavioral and developmental effects of preventing iron deficiency anemia in infancy. Comprehensive information on biological, individual, familial, and environmental factors was obtained in infancy and at 5 and 10 years. The children are now 12–17 years old, an age period when initiation of substance use, especially alcohol and tobacco, is exceptionally high in Chile. From the proposal funded, we list several of the research aims that guide the study to provide readers with a sense of what can be done with longitudinal studies.

Aim 1

The first aim is to characterize individual, familial, and environmental factors from infancy through adolescence that increase or decrease drug involvement in adolescence. The design of the study permits the prospective examination of the unique and joint effects of individual, familial, and environmental factors on increased drug use opportunities and actual drug use.

Aim 2

The second aim is to identify cognitive, behavioral, and social consequences of substance use. By assessing the adolescents at least twice through late adolescence, the study will determine consequences of alcohol, tobacco, or drug use according to levels and patterns of substance use in early adolescence. Consequences will be considered statistically, adjusting for biological, cognitive, and behavioral deficits at infancy, preschool, school age, and middle adolescence.

Aim 3

The third aim is to determine the effects of a probable insult to the dopamine system in infancy (iron deficiency) on substance use and abuse in adolescence. The proposed study provides a unique opportunity to assess the effects of a common early nutritional deficiency on drug use in adolescence. Animal models of iron deficiency anemia in infancy document reduced striatal dopaminergic functioning in adulthood despite iron therapy. Long-term studies in humans point to increased anxiety and depression in early adolescence, impaired function on neurocognitive tasks that involve the dorsolateral prefrontal striatal system, and altered neuroendocrine responses.

The SLS's ability to test this third aim and the corresponding hypotheses is a classic example of interdisciplinary collaboration because investigators from different disciplines, studying different topics, combine their efforts to study a particular problem. In this case, the team includes an investigator who has spent her life understanding the effects of iron deficiency on the brain and on subsequent children's development, along with an investigator who has spent his career studying substance abuse pathways among racial/ethnic minorities. The SLS's findings will contribute to the substance abuse field's understanding of the etiology and prevention of substance use and abuse among youth.

The theoretical model that guides the present work is the life course approach. The life course approach suggests that early life conditions, both biological and social factors, impact later morbidity and mortality (Ben-Shlomo & Kuh, 2002; Halfon & Hochstein, 2002; Krieger, 2001; Kuh & Ben-Schlomo, 1997). That is, exposure to environmental hazards, combined with other hazards, including their accumulation over time, increases the risk of disease over time. In the substance abuse field, environmental hazards can range from the teratogenic effects (effects of substances or agents that can negatively affect embryonic development) of maternal drug use (Autti-Ramo, 2000; Wetherington, Smeriglio, & Finnegan, 1996) to traumatic experiences such as child abuse, among others. Adverse events beginning before birth and continuing through birth and later developmental stages may adversely affect later health by negatively impacting early neurophysiological developments and by increasing the individual's risk of exposure to adverse environmental conditions that accumulate over time. The life course approach is particularly relevant to the experiences of racial/ethnic minority populations, where the disease burden is higher, and in low-income populations, where the number of biological and social insults is larger (either resulting from greater exposure to detrimental living conditions or by having decreased access to care and/or having care of lower quality). These insults may accumulate over time and increase the risk of substance use and progression to abuse. For the present study, we conceptualize risk of substance use as resulting from multiple determinants based on genetic, biological, behavioral, social, and economic contexts that influence one another over time and are reflected in different pathways of risk (Halfon & Hochstein, 2002; Zucker, Boyd, & Howard, 1994). Figure 4.1 illustrates the study's conceptual framework.

In Figure 4.1, it is not possible to show all relationships, including reciprocal ones, that are possible (e.g., parental factors and chronic life stressors may further lead to changes in the brain, which in turn may further increase drug use vulnerability). Rather, we focus the model on associations we propose to test across time. The model displays the potential effect of brain alterations in infancy on the child's temperamental, cognitive, and affective patterns (labeled in the model as

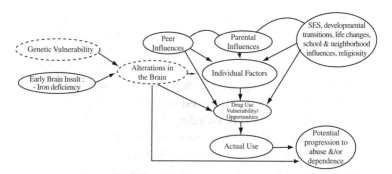

Figure 4.1 Conceptual model of the Santiago Longitudinal Study. Dotted lines indicate constructs not measured in the study. SES refers to socioeconomic status.

"individual factors"), all of which potentially increase drug use opportunities and progression to actual use in later years.

The model also displays the potential effect of peer and parental influences on youth drug use and drug-using opportunities. For example, adolescents living in households with an abusive parent, a parent who suffers from mental illness, or a parent who is abusing substances may grow distant from his or her parents and experience less supervision. Preliminary results seem to indicate that the quality of the relationship of the children with their fathers may be more important than the quality of the relationship with their mothers in helping prevent drug use, independent of the children's sex. Because the role of fathers or male caretakers has generally been neglected in the studies of child development, and of substance abuse in particular, we are not certain about the extent to which this preliminary finding may be a "cultural attribute" found among families in Chile or a more universal pattern. However, we are certain that further research is needed *worldwide* to better understand the role fathers play in their children's development. For example, can fathers provide greater protection, reducing the risk of associating with individuals who have access to drugs, who offer the youth drugs, and who actually use drugs, particularly if they live in neighborhoods where drugs are easier to obtain (Storr, Chen, & Anthony, 2004)? How does the father's religious involvement directly or indirectly reduce the likelihood of his children's drug use (Chen, Dormitzer, Bejarano, & Anthony, 2004; Koenig, Larson, & McCullough, 2001; Steinman & Zimmerman, 2004)? Youth who belong to a denomination that prohibits substance use or that provides clear guidelines under which individuals may consume alcohol, for example, or who are more involved in church and religious activities, may be more likely to adopt attitudes and beliefs that reinforce abstinence or moderate consumption. Simultaneously, these youth might be less likely to associate with drug-consuming peers, further decreasing the likelihood of drug consumption. Furthermore, religious involvement may serve to mediate the stress–drug use association.

Depending on the interplay of these influences over time and based on other individual and environmental factors (e.g., socioeconomic status, developmental transitions, health changes, life stressors), different youth will develop different propensities to encounter drug-using opportunities and to progress to use and abuse. Again, what is the relative role of fathers and mothers in protecting their children? The p study provides substantial data on individual, parental, and family domains from early infancy through mide to late adolescence to test prospectively many of those associations.

The conceptual model also includes the potential long-lasting central nervous system (CNS) effects of early iron deficiency, which may increase the risk of substance use in later years. We are in a unique position to examine pathways by which iron deficiency in early infancy, as well as psychological, behavioral factors, and environmental factors in infancy, childhood, and early adolescence, may influence adolescents' risk of initiating substance use. In this study, however, we do not directly measure alterations to the brain or conduct genetic analyses. As such, the alterations to the brain and genetic vulnerability constructs are presented with dotted lines (see Fig. 4.1). On the other hand, we have data on parental substance use (and that of other household members) for the period when the adolescent was an infant, and at the 5- and 10-year follow-ups. In this study, we will test whether an association exists between parental and familial history of substance use and psychiatric problems and adolescent substance use.

Santiago Longitudinal Study Project Implementation

The first aspect that needs to be mentioned is that the SLS builds on an earlier and ongoing study of the effects of iron deficiency anemia on youth development. Participants (youth and an adult who tends to be the mother primarily) in this longitudinal study had already been assessed when they were infants, at age 5, and at age 10 in conjunction with the iron study, which is funded by the National Institute on Child and Human Development (NICHD). This facilitated the development of the idea that the planning of the SLS could benefit from the prior assessment waves resulting in a 15-year prospective cohort study. The researchers' enthusiasm for this study and the reviewers who after two submissions gave the project a fundable score were based on several key factors. These were as follows: the longitudinal aspect of the study, which would allow for the study of the aims listed above; the comprehensive battery of measures that could be administered to youth and adults; the extensive experience of Dr. Marcela Castillo, a psychologist who is the co-principal investigator in Santiago, managing a large NIH-funded study; and the already established infrastructure to carry out this type of study at her institution, the Institute of Nutrition and Technology of Foods (INTA in Spanish) at the University of Chile.

Essentially, this project's success depends on two levels of communication. The first level consists of the quality of the communication and relationship that the co-investigator and research staff in Chile have established with the study participants. A key aspect of the relationship that the staff in Chile have with the participants stems from the key role that the research conducted at INTA has played historically at addressing health and medical problems, primarily with underserved populations. For example, research conducted at INTA is credited with the elimination of malnutrition in Chile and in other countries. Also, INTA offers quality health care to low-income populations. Hence, gaining entrance into the study participants' lives was facilitated because of *(a)* the participants' positive perception of and relationship with INTA and *(b)* the quality of the relationship participants had had with the research staff for over a decade. In Chapter 2 we described how access to the American Indian populations involved the relationship between the investigator and the tribal leader, tribal council, and elders. In Chapter 3, entrance to the school system involved working with ministers, other governmental leaders, school principals, and teachers. In all cases, access was linked to the quality of the relationship between the investigators and key stakeholders.

The second level is the quality of the communication and relationship between the U.S. research team and the Chilean research team. We first describe what transcribes in Chile and then what transcribes between Chile and the United States.

It goes without saying that the success of the projects depends entirely on the quality of the relationship between the research staff in Chile and the study participants and on the experience of the onsite co-principal investigator managing such a large project. The team in Santiago includes the project's co-principal investigator, a psychologist, the project manager, a nurse, six interviewers, and IT support staff. It also includes an administrative assistant and two drivers. Of these individuals, the co-principal investigator, project manager, three interviewers, the administrative assistant, and one of the drivers already had extensive experience conducting this type of longitudinal study. In addition to having experience contacting participants, scheduling their assessments, and administering the battery of measures, the team had one of the most important qualities necessary for such a project: a positive relationship with study participants. Each one of these individuals has a unique relationship with the youth and parent. The administrative assistant and the van driver make the first contact with the families (which often times needs to be through a home visit because phones are either disconnected or numbers have changed). Then, the driver picks them up at home and brings them to the site at INTA for the assessments. A van was purchased to transport the families. Experience taught us that the alternatives—paying for a cab or bus fare or mileage if the person drives his or her own vehicle—were not going to work for getting the families to the site. These two individuals are key to participants' interest in the study because they are the first faces families see. Some of the mothers (study participants) with jealous husbands have told us that sending the same two staff to make contact with them each year and with a van that has an INTA logo prevented their husbands from questioning their whereabouts, something they feared would have happened if different taxi drivers had been sent to pick them up. Also, this would reduce the likelihood of neighbors wondering where she and her son were going; after all, they were going to INTA. This is an important example of being sensitive to the needs of some of the mothers who expressed fears of their jealous husbands or boyfriends.

The hiring of local interviewers who can understand the lives of the population under investigation and who may have shared experiences (being a mother of an adolescent, having experienced unemployment) are critical elements of the success of this study. Additional sensitivities consist of presenting the study as a partnership between the U.S. and Chilean investigators. Also, as indicated earlier, INTA is a well-known entity in Chile. It is a research institute that played a mayor role in the eradication of malnutrition in Chile and in the development and evaluation of similar programs in other Latin American countries. It is an organization that is respected by the communities where the families in our study come from. The van has INTA's logo on its door, which allows for easy maneuvering in the communities.

Once the families arrive at INTA, the nurse explains the study and administers the consent form to both the parent and child. Once consent is obtained, she measures and weighs the children, does a physical exam, a pubertal examination, and draws blood for the iron analyses. As a side note, we also request permission to conduct genetic analyses using the blood drawn. In the future, we should be able to conduct analyses of gene–environment interactions. Subsequently the youth meets with one interviewer, and the parent (or adult) with another interviewer in separate, private rooms. These assessments last 2 hours and consist of the administration of a battery of measures to both the youth and the parent (or other adult). Because the study intended to measure characteristics of the mother, due to space and time limitations only a few questions were included about other family members. However, in the pilot testing stage of the questionnaire, two issues surfaced that resulted in our modifying the instrument. One was that several mothers requested that we also include detailed questions about the consumption of alcohol and other substances by other family members, mainly the child's dad. They indicated that although they themselves may not consume substances at all or in very small amounts and very sporadically, that many in their families, mostly but not only males, consumed alcohol in large amounts. They wanted to be able to tell this aspect of their lives so that we could examine how these individuals may have an impact on the child's life. To add these questions we had to cut another section, but we did so out of sensitivity to the study participants. Fortunately, we believe our study was strengthened by these changes. Another change had to do with the approximately 10% of caregivers who are not mothers. Again, the questionnaire was designed to ask detailed questions about the mothers, and after the revisions it asked about the consumption of substances by other family members. What should be done when a grandmother, a nanny, an older sibling, or an aunt brings the child to INTA to participate in the study, as was the case for about 10% of participants? Collecting detailed data about these individuals was still done with the caveat that they play a role in the youth development. In the analyses we will examine whether the responses from these 10% differ from the rest of the sample. Out of respect for the families, the time they were taking to bring the child to INTA, and the mothers' schedules, it was not appropriate to insist that the mother be the one to bring the child. Rather than resorting to this, we would simply not have the child show up.

At all stages, study participants are treated with the utmost respect and everything possible is done to maintain confidentiality. In the section "Human Subjects Protection," we describe this process in greater detail. In the past, in the iron deficiency study parents were provided with the results of their childrne's physical, emotional, and cognitive development and were given suggestions on how to talk with their doctors if a nutritional deficiency was found and how to communicate with the child's teacher if a certain deficiency was identified by the cognitive assessments. Parents found this information very beneficial. Unfortunately, for the substance abuse study, the nature of the study inquiring about illegal behaviors and given the age of the youth (all participants are in pre-adolescence or adolescence), it is no longer possible to disclose to parents results of the assessments unless the youth is contemplating harming himself or herself, has tried suicide before, plans to hurt someone else, or reports being a victim of abuse. This is made very clear to the parent and youth in the consent process. Instead, we provide parents with a generic sheet with information about challenges adolescents experience and ways that parents can better communicate with them. We also encourage parents to seek help from their doctors, community organizations, the clergy, school counselors, and others if they find their child has begun using drugs. Finally, as a way to thank them for their participation the youth are given movie tickets, and the adults are given a scarf or mittens.

The second level is the quality of the communication and relationship between the U.S. research team and the Chilean research team. This is mainly done by maintaining nearly daily communication between the project manager in the United States and the co-principal investigator and research staff in Chile and by at least weekly communication between the principal investigator in the United States and the co-principal investigator in Chile. All of this communication is done by email, internet via SKYPE (http://www.skype.com/), or phone as necessary. There is also considerable traveling of U.S. personnel to Chile. Additional communication is maintained by a network of individuals who travel to Chile or individuals who travel to the United States. For example, some of these individuals are students selected to participate in the Minority Health and Institutional Research Training (MHIRT), an NIH-Fogarty training program at the University of Michigan. This program provides a year-long research training that culminates with a 3-month hands-on research experience in a foreign country. Students interested in working in the project in Santiago spend three summer months in Chile. This allows for additional "in-person" communication between the research teams. Another example is that of a medical epidemiologist from the University of Chile, who came to the

University of Michigan to do a month-long research internship. This individual became an additional node between the U.S. and Chilean teams. Also, a U.S. doctoral student has traveled repeatedly to Chile to conduct qualitative interviews with the families to obtain richer data. For all intents and purposes, these individuals serve as an "extension" and additional "nodes," if you will, of the U.S. and Chilean research teams, substantially helping to improve the communication between the groups. As we describe in the earlier chapters, developing and maintaining quality relationships among people with varied perspectives and interests is one of the most important factors to successfully carry out a research project. Careful attention is paid by the U.S. investigators at how they interact with their Chilean counterparts. All attempts are made to avoid dictating or imposing a decision on them. In fact, most decisions are made jointly after several discussions. On occasions when a decision needs to be made and time constraints make it impossible to discuss the matter, the decision is made and then soon thereafter it is discussed. This is a process that works both ways. The Chilean team may have to make a decision, and then this is discussed with the principal investigator, and the potential next steps are jointly discussed and decided. Another form of respectful interaction is to decide on the methodology and the budget jointly, and then to provide the Chilean team with complete freedom on whom they hire, how staff are supervised, and how the day-to-day operations are handled. Also, every single report, manuscript, and conference presentation has been worked on jointly with the Chilean collaborator and for some of the work we have invited some of the staff to collaborate as authors. For the Chilean staff, being an author on a report, publication, or presentation is not important for their career. However, they have appreciated the invitation and as one person said, "It provides proof I was part of this big project after so many years of working on it."

For these activities to work well, of course, the project needs to have a trusted and experienced manager. This would be the case with any study, but there are larger repercussions in a foreign country, given the distance. Additional considerations that work in building and sustaining a positive relationship include speaking a "common" language—not only the spoken language (Spanish in this case) but also sharing common values or respecting the differences and being open to considering differences.

Human Subjects Protection

Unlike the anonymous cross-sectional survey described earlier, for this longitudinal study it is important to obtain identifying information to be able to link the participants' information over time. This requirement adds a critical level of care that one must have when conducting these studies. All the traditional precautions have been taken, including being very clear with the parents and children about the purpose of the study and the activities they will be asked to participate in (including the urine tests and blood samples to be drawn from the youth). It is also made very clear that they can refuse to answer any question, refuse to do anything in the study (i.e., refuse the urine test), and that they can withdraw from the study at any time without any consequences whatsoever. Participants who declined participation are not contacted again out of respect for their decision. In one case, an adolescent decided to stop answering the questions midway through; this was treated as a completely acceptable decision.

If there is anything that is unfortunate about this process, however, it is the length of the consent form, which is over 12 pages. The reason for this is the use of a template form that is utilized by the Institutional Review Board (IRB) at the Medical School of the sponsoring University. This template tends to be 9–10 pages longer than the consent forms utilized in the social sciences but because the purpose of this study is not to make changes to the IRB forms and IRB procedures, we work with what we have. The IRB in Chile expressed some concern about the length of the form but because of the thoroughness of the information covered, they did not ask that it be shortened. Due to the length of the consent forms, the research staff reads the consent along with the parent and youth and spends time discussing it and the participants' options. Please note that this criticism of the IRB forms is by no means a criticism of the importance of the need for researchers to carefully attend to human subjects' protection issues. All of the authors support the mission of IRBs, and in fact, one of the authors is an IRB member, and the Chilean co-investigator is an IRB member at the University of Chile. However, there are many aspects of the IRB process that need to be examined more critically and potentially changed.

Returning now to our discussion of the implementation of the project, in order to collect the best possible data and to further protect participants' confidentiality in a foreign country, we initially implemented the use of direct, wireless, data entry with tablet PCs. Direct data entry with tablet PCs follows the strategy used with computer-assisted personal interviews (CAPI) or computer-assisted self-interviews (CASI). CAPI consists of interviewing the participant and then the interviewer enters the responses into the computer. With CASI, the procedure is the same as CAPI except the individuals enter the answers to the questions into the computers themselves. Regardless of who enters the data, these data are saved automatically into a device. The device can be a desktop, laptop, tablet PC, or a handheld tool. The data can also be saved directly into a secure server through wireless connection instead of saving data into the device itself. Only selected staff can have access to the server, which is monitored daily.

The preferred strategy is the wireless data collection option for storage in a secure server as opposed to the device being used to collect the data. The idea of using a tablet PC is to mimic the use of a notebook to write, something individuals are accustomed to, as opposed to having to look at an open screen. With the use of a special pen, the person can scroll up and down and click to answer questions. The person can even write into it as well. For the SLS, seven tablet PCs were purchased, a wireless network was put in place, a server purchased and installed at the evaluation site, INTA, and the questionnaires programmed to function in the tablet PC for direct data entry. Unfortunately, we were not able to get the system to work for direct data entry. Some of the problems we encountered included the server malfunctioning in unexpected ways, some of the tablet PCs behaving capriciously (freezing, sometimes not saving data), and slow connection to the network via the Internet. In addition, the research staff who are conducting the interviews fear that something will go wrong with the tablet PCs, the server, or the building's electricity, which will result in the interruption of the assessment and subsequent loss of data. Another concern is that once the participant has answered a question and the data have been entered, it is not possible to know if a data-entering mistake has been made unless the interviewer or participant recognizes it immediately or later *and* is motivated to go back to change the answer. Being sensitive to the needs of the staff, we decided to suspend data collection with the tablets PC. Instead, the staff uses them to enter data after the assessment is completed. For this purpose, the use of this technology has worked very well.

Interestingly, after attempting to implement cutting-edge technology for the purpose of data collection, we in the research team are not entirely convinced of their superiority when compared to the simpler and potentially outdated paper-and-pencil methods and interviewer-administered measures. Collecting data with paper and pencil allows the interviewers to go through the questionnaire more quickly because it is easier for them to read and mark the answers on paper. It permits for more rapport with the participants. It also allows them to easily correct mistakes if one is identified, particularly if one needs to return to a question asked 30 minutes earlier or 20 pages back in the questionnaire. The use of paper and pencil allows the interviewer to write observations on the side of the page or below a question concerning a comment the participant may have made that can later inform the answers. Interviewers are also happy to have a hard copy of the completed instrument to be able to refer to at a later time. Another positive aspect of using paper and pencil is that it was sensitive to individuals who are illiterate, had lower literacy levels, or who were uncomfortable with the use of machines. These issues mainly affected adults because youth are quite computer literate. Demonstrating sensitivity on these issues was also helpful in preventing caretakers from not participating in the study.

There is also a protocol in place for collecting urine specimens in an attempt to validate the youth responses to cigarette, alcohol, marijuana, pasta base (unprocessed cocaine), and cocaine use. Numerous biological procedures, such as hair, urine, blood, saliva, and sweat analysis, are available, and each strategy has its pros and cons (Cone, 1997). Of all the various biological possibilities (Cone, 1997), the choices were narrowed to hair testing and urine testing. Unfortunately, utilizing both strategies was cost prohibitive, even though it would have allowed for the conduct of an important validation study. After conducting a thorough literature review and from discussions with a number of investigators in the United States and toxicologists from the University of Chile's Antidoping Center, we settled on using urine tests. We learned that the validity of hair testing is affected by the length and texture of the person's hair. Although urine tests have a more limited detection time, the technology is mature, the cutoff points are well defined, standards for testing are well established, and the potential for contaminations are less than with hair testing, unless the individual purposely sets out to "beat" the test, but that would be the case with any other test as well. On the other hand, hair testing allows for the detection of drug metabolites for a longer period of time but is not well suited to detect marijuana, the technology is still undergoing considerable refinement, it has high potential for environmental contamination, and participants would need to have sufficient hair length.

In pilot testing, the biggest concern among youth was not being able to urinate when asked to give the specimen or saying "but I just went to the bathroom before coming here." Other than that, the youth did not express other concerns. We believe the reason for this is the positive relationships the staff have with the families, which as we indicated earlier, have been built over the years.

The study initially called for urine analyses to be conducted on 50% of a randomly selected group of youth. The budget would not allow for more. However, when the project was funded, it experienced a 12% cut and subsequently the budget has been affected by the devaluation of the dollar, monetary fluctuations that need to be considered with international projects. Therefore, a decision was made to test only 5% of the youth. Before describing the steps taken to obtain the urine sample, we indicate why a decision was made to test 5% of the youth. The reader may be aware of a strategy called "bogus pipeline" (Aguinis & Henle, 2001). The bogus pipeline consists of telling a study participant that a particular procedure will be conducted to elicit more honest answers to survey questions, thus deceiving the participant. For example, immediately after completing the questionnaire youth would be asked to give a urine sample to validate their responses to the questions about drugs. But the urine would not be collected, or it would be collected following all the formal proceduresonly to be discarded without the youth's knowledge. The urine specimen could also be collected prior to questionnaire administration in order to reinforce the importance of the individual answering the questions about drug use honestly. However, this strategy involves deception, which would mean there would need to be a debriefing period afterward to tell the study participants about this bogus strategy. The research team decided it would not be appropriate to use deception with adolescents because issues of trust are critical when dealing with adolescents. However, it was decided that by keeping the disclosure in the consent form that a small sample of youth would be selected randomly to provide a urine sample, we could still encourage youth to answer as honestly as possible. In this way, we could encourage honesty without deception. Also, as mentioned earlier, youth and parents are reminded that youth who do not want to do this can skip out of it with no consequences whatsoever in the same manner that they can decide not to answer any question in the questionnaires. Nonetheless, we believe that for some youth the idea that they may be randomly selected to give urine will encourage them to be more honest in their responses. This strategy does not prevent youth from gambling that they will not be selected to provide a urine sample and lying about their drug use. There is nothing one can do about this.

The questionnaire also includes a measure of social desirability, a short form of the Marlowe-Crowne Social Desirability Scale (Reynolds, 1982). Data from individuals who score above a particular range will be scrutinized more carefully for inconsistencies and potentially deleted from analyses if their responses are unclear. There is no exact science for determining whether an individual is answering in a more socially desirable manner (for either under-reporting or over-reporting drug use), particularly in a foreign country, whereby the way social desirability is expressed by youth in other countries is likely to differ from that in the United States. In fact, preliminary analyses of this scale reflect substantially different response patterns than U.S. populations. We have decided that before we use this measure in our analyses, we will seek a substantial amount of validation. Perhaps more important than this scale, however, are a positive relationship with the interviewer, the privacy afforded at INTA in the interview room, and the trust that parents will not be told of their answers. These primary factors will encourage youth to disclose sensitive information.

Questionnaire Construction

Creating an instrument that captured all the constructs the teams wanted to assess within a 2-hour period was not easy. It is true that numerous measures of substance use, abuse, and dependence exist, and that different measures of mental-health constructs, parenting, and family relationships, among others, with adequate validity and reliability also exist. But because of their large numbers and differences in strengths and weaknesses, appropriateness for different populations, research designs, and research questions, selecting the measures was an extremely difficult task. Anyone who has ever put a battery of questions together understands this difficulty. In fact, one of the authors of this book participated in a large NIH-funded initiative led by RTI International to contribute to the integration of standard measures from multiple domains for use in genetics and epidemiologic research around the world. This project, with funding from the National Human Genome Research Institute (NHGRI), came about in recognition of the need for more consistency in the selection and utilization of measures, and operationalization of constructs, across studies to facilitate and encourage cross-study comparisons and analysis (for more details see http://www.phenx.org).

In the SLS, it took over 6 months of diligent work to compile and narrow down the list. This was done by the principal investigator in consultation with the co-principal investigator in Chile and with numerous colleagues worldwide. Once the battery of measures was put together, these had to be translated into Spanish. Fortunately, a few of the measures already existed in Spanish (i.e., CBCL), but these still had to be checked for their appropriateness with the Chilean populations.

Over 900 questions and their response categories were translated for the youth battery of questions and over 800 for the parent's battery. This work was done by the project's PI and a number of volunteers. Due to funding constraints the project could not hire a translator to do this work. In fact, it is not uncommon for the translation task to fall on the foreign collaborator because funds are often insufficient to hire a professional translator. Because the principal investigator's native language is Spanish, he did not want to burden the co-principal investigator in Chile with this task. Interestingly, after the study had begun, the co-principal investigator expressed her gratitude to the principal investigator for not passing along (or "dumping") this task on her.

Once the measures were translated, there was no time to translate all of them back into English. Instead, during the translation, extensive communication took place about each question and response category between the project's principal and co-principal investigators in Chile. Subsequently, the instrument was reviewed by three of the interviewers (research staff) at which point more changes were made. Finally, the questionnaire was pilot tested with 30 families and further changes made. Subsequently, as the questionnaire has been administered, a few more changes have been made based on issues that have surfaced over time. All these changes are carefully recorded.

In addition to the changes made to the questionnaire per the mothers' requests described earlier, the following are three additional examples. Each of these demonstrates the timely, bilingual, and sensitive nature of the collaboration between team members in two countries that was needed to ensure that questionnaire items were appropriate for Chilean youth.

Example 1

During one of the regular meetings between the research staff at INTA, the research site in Santiago, Chile, questions and uncertainties surfaced about words and phrases used in some of the items in a questionnaire administered to youth. This was made known to the project coordinator in Michigan via an e-mail in Spanish stating the above. The e-mail included an attachment detailing the items in question and the team's suggestions to modify the items. The coordinator, fluent in Spanish, then promptly replied to the e-mail, notifying the interviewers that she would contact the principal investigator to review the document attached and consider their suggestions. The coordinator contacted the principal investigator minutes after receiving the e-mail and set up a time to meet with the principal investigator the following day to review the document. The document prepared by the research staff was clear and easy to follow. Each item was stated as it appeared on the questionnaire, followed by the teams' suggestions as to how it might be restated, reworded, and so forth, and it ended with an explanation of how the item created confusion to either the interviewer or the youth interviewee. One of the suggestions included changes to two words used in the Positive and Negative Affect Schedule (PANAS) (Watson, Clark, & Tellegen, 1988), a 20-item self-report measure of positive and negative affect, that according to them, the youth were having difficulty comprehending. The instructions read "Next, we are interested in some of the ways you feel, on the average. Following is a list of words that describe different feelings and emotions. After I read each word I will ask you if you feel like this 'Very slightly or not at all,' 'A little,' 'Moderately,' 'Quite a bit,' or 'Extremely.'" The interviewers explained that the word *excited* was being associated with sexuality, and they thought that the word could be replaced with a synonym such as *agitado* or *apasionado*, which in English translate into *agitated* or *passionate*, respectively. The principal investigator, Chilean co-principal investigator, and research coordinator reviewed the English version of the measure and noted that the word *excited* was being used in a positive context with a meaning similar to being animated, happy, or enthusiastic, or *animado, contento,* and *entusiasmado* in Spanish. The principal investigator discussed this interpretation with the research team. After more discussion, the research staff conducting the assessments were asked to select the word they thought would be most appropriate. The team went on to select the word *apasionado*, a word with a positive connotation.

The second word, *hostile or Hostil,* in Spanish, was generally unknown to the youth participants. The staff suggested that *agresivo* (or *aggressive* in English) might be a word more widely known by the youth. The principal investigator , co-principal investigator in Chile, and the project coordinator agreed that a hostile individual did not necessarily have to be an aggressive individual. They referred to an English thesaurus for possible synonyms for *hostile* and found such words as *antagonistic* (or *antagonista* in Spanish), which they proposed as a possible replacement. After further discussion with the team, the research staff suggested that they would prefer to replace the word *hostile* with the word *defensive* (or *defensivo* in Spanish). The research staff indicated that they would prefer not to use the term *antagonista* because in their experience, *antagonistic* was not generally used in everyday language in Chile. They argued that using this word would create confusion about its meaning for the youth and lead the interviewers to have to intervene by explaining the meaning of the word to the youth, which was occurring with *hostile*. They also indicated that *antagonistic* was more commonly used in literature and that the youth were likely to associate the words with a villain, or the "bad guy" in a movie. They wrote the following:

Básicamente la palabra "antagonista" no es muy utilizada en el habla cotidiana y caeríamos en el mismo problema de tener que explicar que significa. "Antagonista" es usada más que nada en jerga literaria y muy probablemente se asocie a "ser el malo de la película" por parte de los adolescentes.

Basically, the word *antagonistic* is not commonly used and we would end up with the same problem of having to explain what it means. *Antagonistic* is used in the literary world and the adolescents would likely associate it with "the bad guy in the movie."

Example 2

A second suggestion made by the interviewers referred to the phrasing of interviewer instructions on a scale on youths' general opinions on cigarette use taken from an established instrument on cigarette use. The instructions read "Please tell me how much you agree or disagree with the following statements." In Spanish, "*¿Me podrías decir cúan de acuerdo o en desacuerdo estás con las siguientes afirmaciones?*" The interviewers felt that the current instructions conveyed an assumption that the youth was a smoker. After discussing this point with a group of youth, to reduce youth perception of interviewer assumptions, the team wanted to change the instructions to read "*What is your opinion about the following statements, even if you don't smoke?*" In Spanish, "*¿Qué opinas respecto de las siguientes afirmaciones, aunque tú no fumes?*" The interviewers had already suggested this change to their supervisor in Chile during the regular meeting, and the supervisor was okay with this suggestion. She was aware that the interviewers had a very acute sense of how the youth were interpreting the instructions and responding to questions because of their extensive experience interviewing this group of youth. The principal investigator and the coordinator in Michigan trusted, valued, and agreed with the interviewers' suggestions to modify these instructions.

Example 3

On another occasion, the project coordinator who is based in the United States, a Mexican immigrant whose command of the English and Spanish languages is superb, suggested that some changes be made to the response categories of a measure of youth perceptions of their physical appearance. In a section on physical appearance youth were asked to tell the interviewer the following: "How tall are you?" "How tall do you wish you could be right now?" "How much do you weigh," and "How much do you wish you could weigh?" The response option consisted of asking youth to provide a number in meters and centimeters (or kilograms for weight) or by answering "don't know." It was discovered that youth were having difficulty giving a precise number and would tend to respond in more general terms, such as "more," "less," "the same," and even asking the interviewer, "What should it be?" The interviewers wrote the following:

Creemos que es importante, si se pudiera, agregar estas alternativas porque es una situación frecuente el que los lolos te contesten que están bien o que les gustaría pesar o medir lo mismo que ahora. Esto es distinto a no sé.

We believe it is important, if possible, to add these alternatives because it is a situation where the youth answer that they are fine or that they would like to weigh or measure the same as what they are now. These are different [responses] from "don't know."

Hence, as a result of this observation and the youth feedback, response categories were added to capture these types of answers. Youth who could provide a value could still do so, but now those who could not had an option. It is interesting to note that these three examples of modifications made to the instrument came about after the translations had occurred and the instrument pilot was tested with youth and parents. It reflects the need for ongoing vigilance about modifications that may need to be made to an ongoing project. It is also a good example about the importance of listening to study participants and maintaining open communication among staff and investigators and between staff and principal investigators.

An additional component of the SLS is a Systematic Neighborhood Evaluation of *manzanas,* or neighborhood blocks. This instrument was designed with the characteristics of Chilean neighborhoods in mind. In this chapter we do not describe how this instrument was created due to space limitations. Suffice it to say that the process involved several years of design, pilot testing, and refining. With the exception of some of the items utilized to evaluate neighborhoods (i.e., lack of abandoned buildings), we are hesitant to make any statements about the extent to which these modifications reflect elements of the Chilean culture or are sample specific. We are confident in saying, however, that these changes are sensitive to the developmental stage of the youth and their lives, take into consideration the feedback given to investigators by the child and his or her parents, and serve as another illustration of being responsive to observations made by frontline staff. These changes certainly helped improve the study.

Data Considerations in Longitudinal Studies

Due to the large number of measures and data available, and the complexity of the conceptual model, key selected examples are utilized to illustrate the SLS analytic plan. First, the plan takes advantage of the repeated measures. Hypotheses testing will occur sequentially, beginning with simple models, then move to analyses of increasing complexity. Because many of the predictor variables are correlated, it is expected that some variables will be selected or composite indicators will be formed (through factor analysis or by developing latent variables to describe the overarching trait or environmental system). Due to the variability within the same wave, the variability in the spacing of waves, and the variability in the number of waves per respondent due to attrition, age is a better variable, instead of wave, to utilize as the unit of time in most analyses (Mehta & West, 2000). The SLS relies on traditional techniques such as ANOVA, multiple regression, MANOVA, and MANCOVA to address questions about linear relations of variables at single time points. Whenever appropriate, multilevel mixed models will be utilized to account for the non-independence in the data when previous and parent data are included in analyses. Hierarchical liner models (HLM), hierarchical generalized linear models (HGLM), latent growth models (LGM), growth mixture modeling (GMM), and general growth mixture modeling (GGMM) will be the major techniques to examine longitudinal data. The statistical basis of LGM estimation is derived from structural equation modeling (SEM). Whereas traditional SEM focuses entirely on the covariance structure of the observed variables, LGM analyzes both the mean structure and the covariance structure (Meredith & Tisak, 1990; Muthén, 2001; Muthén & Muthén, 2000; Raudenbush, Bryk, Cheong, & Congdon, 2004; Willet & Sayer, 1994).

Thus, data will be analyzed at two levels: Level 1, the within-subject model, and Level 2, the between-subject model. In the Level 1 model, each youth growth trajectory is estimated. The dependent variables are observations at various time points (e.g., alcohol use over three time points). The initial status (intercept of the growth trajectory) and the rate of change (slope of the growth trajectory) are represented as latent factors in the model. In the Level 2 model, these latent factors become the dependent variables. The effects of the independent variables on these trajectories are estimated. The GMM combines LGM and latent class growth analyses. It estimates different growth curve shapes associated with the latent classes and provides information of posterior probabilities of class membership for all participants. The GMM also allows variation around the mean growth curve in each latent class (Muthén & Muthén, 2000). The GGMM provides a flexible statistical framework to allow for the estimation of the association among different trajectories classes, their antecedents, and their consequences (Muthén & Muthén, 2000). We have also began to analyze the data with item response theory (IRT) and confirmatory factor analyses in order to examine how items "behave" depending on the children's sex and age.

In this chapter we do not provide examples of power analyses because this topic was covered in detail in Chapter 3. One difference for this longitudinal design, however, is that power analyses need to take into account the dependency that occurs from measurement across time. In the cross-sectional study in Latin America, the dependency or clustering had to do with the lack of independence due to the cluster sample. In longitudinal studies, the lack of independence has to do with repeated observations, though it could also be related to clustering if, for instance, the sample was drawn from units (i.e., schools, block groups, clinics, hospitals, community centers) that would include more or less homogenous elements (i.e., children).

Next we describe two specific components of the longitudinal study of PTSD in Detroit, Michigan (http://detroitneighborhoodhealthstudy. org/) that we believe will be of particular interest to readers.

THE DETROIT NEIGHBORHOOD HEALTH STUDY

The Detroit Neighborhood Health Study (DNHS), a study funded by the National Institute on Drug Abuse and the National Institute of Mental Health, focuses on ecological factors (e.g., concentrated disadvantage, income distribution, residential segregation, the quality of the built environment) that might influence individual PTSD and substance use. We highlight two innovative aspects of this study. One is the use of biomarkers to assess compromised immunological functioning in population studies. The second is a discussion of personnel issues when conducting systematic neighborhood assessments that include a combination of university students and community residents.

Assessing Compromised Immunology

An important component of the DNHS is to examine whether ecologic stressors are associated with compromised immunological functioning.[1] To study this research question, immunological and inflammatory markers will be utilized. This aspect of the DNHS study is under the direction of Dr. Allison Aiello, assistant professor of epidemiology at the Center for Social Epidemiology and Population Health at the University of Michigan. Dr. Aiello's work aims to reduce racial and social disparities in viral and bacterial diseases linked to chronic diseases. Considering that other researchers have found that psychosocial and physical stressors trigger increased antibody response to latent herpesviruses, including Epstein-Barr virus (EBV) and cytomegalovirus (CMV) (Kennedy, 1996), she posits that the biological pathway by which stressors may lead to an increased humoral mediated antibody response is through the down-regulation of cellular immunity.

It is possible to study this question because herpesvirus antibody levels, for example, have been shown to be among the most consistent immunological markers of stress (Herbert & Cohen, 1993), and EBV and CMV are extremely ubiquitous in adult populations. The prevalence of latent infection for these two viruses is estimated at 90%–100% (de Jong et al., 1998; Henle & Henle, 1982). Generally acquired in childhood, these viruses are carried throughout life since there are no treatments that can eradicate these latent infections. In this study, blood is being drawn to measure the presence of these viruses in order to analyze the extent to which these are associated with ecological stressors. This unique aspect of the DNHS study highlights the importance of measuring not only psychological and social constructs but also biological ones to better understand how people navigate their environments. It is also important to note that we encountered countless individuals who said people in Detroit, and particularly African Americans, will not agree to provide a blood sample due to the historical distrust that Detroit residents have toward academic researchers. In preparation for this situation, we hired community nurses from the Visiting Nurses Association working in Detroit. We are pleased to say that participation is going extremely well. What is important to highlight here, once again, is the relationship and trust present that allowed us to gain entrance into the participants' lives. Using the same consent forms and script, but with project staff not known among community residents, we would have had a much more difficult time conducting the study. The lesson we offer here is that it is important to acknowledge these historical facts and to plan on handling them with sensitivity. In this case, one aspect of being sensitive meant hiring nurses from the communities we intended to include in the study.

When the Academic and "Real" Worlds Meet

The second aspect we wanted to highlight from the DNHS concerns the dynamics that took place when conducting the Neighborhood Systematic Assessments between eight undergraduate and graduate students and 13 Detroit community residents. These individuals were hired to conduct systematic assessments of 138 block groups from 54 Detroit neighborhoods over the course of 6 weeks in the summer of 2008. There were many challenges with two groups of people from very different backgrounds. However, as we were placed together to achieve a common goal, the challenges were met with success. Figure 4.2 lists the some of the challenges (Momper & Nordberg, 2008).

- Logistics:
  - locating safe, convenient and accessible restrooms in Detroit
  - having available drivers with experience driving in a city
  - scheduling of personnel
  - adequate pairing of data collectors to take into account safety issues, knowledge of the neighborhood, walking speed, ability to read maps, and knowledge of the survey instrument
  - route mapping that takes into account the speed of the walkers and the drop off and pick-up points

- Fear
  - of neighborhoods by students
  - of poverty by students
  - of not being paid on time by Detroit residents who were not trusting of a bureaucracy
  - of packs of dogs by both students and residents
  - of neighborhood residents by students

- Differences
  - Age
  - Gender
  - Socio-economic status
  - Race and ethnicity
  - Life experience
  - Education
  - Dialect
  - Privilege
  - Knowledge of Detroit

- Discomforts
  - Walking and driving in hot and/or stormy weather
  - Cramped vans
  - Personality conflicts

Figure 4.2 Examples of challenges when the academic world and "real" world meet.

These challenges were successfully overcome as both the students and the Detroit residents became more aware of both the daily needs of the group and of the project to be able to achieve project completion in a thorough, efficient manner. Below we provide some examples of how the group evolved and cooperated with one another:

1. *Awareness.* Everyone became aware of the daily route to the neighborhoods and looked for restrooms and inexpensive places to dine.
2. *Strategic collaboration.* Van assignments were made with the knowledge of who worked well together in terms of personalities, physical abilities, and survey skills (e.g., a good map reader was paired with someone who was a good assessor of the neighborhood).
3. *Incentives.* Agreements were made at the start of the day, or during the day, to complete certain block groups in a timely manner to avoid the heat or inclement weather.
4. *Unity.* The vans always stayed together in the neighborhoods, and the surveyors worked in pairs.
5. *Safety.* Students learned to respect the instincts and the knowledge of the community residents regarding potential dangers. Students were paired with community residents, or males were paired with females.
6. *Health.* We had an ample supply of water, air-conditioned vans were available for the surveyors, and we built in more breaks for the elders and less physically able people.
7. *Flexibility.* The group agreed to drop people off in their home neighborhoods after work if they lived nearby, as not all people had transportation. We discussed lunch options and made concessions about where and when we would eat.
8. *Cultural sensitivity.* Students became aware that some of their Detroit colleagues lived in underserved neighborhoods; thus, they became more careful about making comments about the condition of a neighborhood.
9. *Empowerment.* Detroit residents became aware that their "street" knowledge was as valuable as the students' "book" knowledge. Several Detroit residents became motivated to go back to college as a result of their positive interactions with the college students.

10. *Professionalism*. Both the students and the residents developed styles of their own when interacting with neighborhood residents; they exuded a sense of professionalism and were aware that they represented the University.

This is not to say that personality conflicts did not occur or that racial issues did not arise. They did. However, the group members were able to transcend their differences in order to complete the project. We are pleased to report that as the group became increasingly cohesive, any outside issues affecting any one member became something they, as a group, wanted to overcome together. The ability of the two groups of people to successfully complete the project and be personally proud of what they had done was the result of mutual cooperation that bridged the gap that often occurs between academia and the "real world."

CONCLUSION

In this chapter we describe critical aspects of two longitudinal studies currently underway with diverse populations. The Santiago Longitudinal Study highlighted the importance of building trusting and long-lasting relationships between investigators and between investigators and participants in order to successfully implement a project. This chapter also highlighted innovative data collection techniques, human subjects' protection issues, and advanced data analytic approaches, as well as the challenges of doing research in an international setting. It also provided extensive illustrations of research that is sensitive to the characteristics of the population. Although initially designed as a standard quantitative study, in the first 2 years of the project we have also conducted two embedded qualitative studies. In the first study, 31 randomly selected families representing the various *comunas* (neighborhoods) participated in a semi-structure interviewed with open- and close-ended questions about the quality of life, neighborhood characteristics, violence, coping with challenges adolescents face, help-seeking behavior, and so forth. From this study we identified some interesting differences on substance use and domestic violence as a function of place of residence. Differences on these behaviors were noted between whether families living in *pasajes* (passage ways) versus those living on main streets (Sanchez, Delva, & Castillo, 2007). We also conducted a standardized systematic assessment of the neighborhood blocks where these families reside, thus acquiring more important contextual data. A year later we conducted a follow-up qualitative study that consisted of in-depth interviews with 11 of the parents to explore in greater depth these uncovered themes (Horner, Sanchez, Castillo, & Delva, 2008). This subsequent study served to explain and expand on these initial findings. In this qualitative study, the concepts of *los delincuentes* (the delinquents) emerged, a concept that blamed criminal activity to some outside (outside from their neighborhood) delinquent identity, a concept we have not seen in the literature (Horner, Sanchez, Castillo, & Delva, in press). We mention these qualitative studies because they show how different research methods can be added into a study and how the application of multiple research methods, as described in Chapter 2, can tremendously enhance one's understanding of a phenomenon.

The second study, a longitudinal study of PTSD was used as an example of the importance of collecting biological data, in this case assessing compromised immunological functioning, to complement a psychosocial approach and to do so in a way that takes into account community residents' distrust. From this study we also provided examples of the tension that arose when university students were paired with community residents when conducting a systematic assessment of neighborhood blocks. We discussed some of these challenges and the ways these were successfully handled.

5

Use of Experimental Designs in Community Settings

I n this chapter we illustrate how a two-armed randomized clinical trial (RCT) was designed and implemented with low-income African American women who were mothers of young children (under 6 years of age) living in the most impoverished areas in Detroit. For details on the strength and weaknesses of quasi-experimental and experimental designs, readers are encouraged to read the classics by Campbell and Stanley (1966) and by Cook and Campbell (1979).

This study was conducted using a combined etic–emic approach, whereby the emic component (essentially the tailoring of the intervention) became more, if not entirely, driven by socioeconomic status considerations and gender issues, given that the intervention protocol called for the recruitment of biological mothers and other female caregivers. The study was less driven by African American cultural elements because the study participants were among the most economically disadvantaged populations in the United States In this study, being sensitive to the study participants was less about being sensitive to potentially stereotypical cultural elements about African Americans and more about being sensitive to the challenges, if not outright traumatic and unacceptable experiences, that severely economically disadvantaged populations face. For example, impoverished families tend to live in neighborhoods where healthier foods (i.e., fresh fruits and vegetables) are substantially less likely to be available than in more affluent neighborhoods; furthermore, a family may not be able to afford these items, even if they are available. In this study, sensitivity toward the study population involved paying closer attention to the structural and economic conditions surrounding their lives, rather than African American cultural aspects.

The purpose of this particular study was to conduct an RCT to test the effectiveness of a multimodal intervention to enhance oral health. Because enhanced oral health is affected by many factors, including a person's socioeconomic position (e.g., issues concerning access to dental care and to optimal nutrition) and mental health, the intervention was designed to address these. Designing an intervention that could address these multiple factors simultaneously is a good example of how intersectionality of multiple identities can be taken into consideration when conducting intervention research—a perspective we propose should be incorporated by cross-cultural researchers (see discussion in Chapter 7).

This study was funded by the National Institute on Dental and Craniofacial Research (NIDCR). In this chapter we describe what guided the formulation of the research question(s), the theoretical model, and the development and implementation of the project. Due to space limitations and to maintain the focus on the development of the intervention, in this chapter we do not discuss the data-analytic strategies utilized. However, based on the complex sampling design and the longitudinal component, we mention that appropriate approaches are being utilized to analyze these types of correlated data, similar to those described in the earlier chapters.

The study's aim to improve oral health among low-income African American families and their children arose from the recognition that there are considerable disparities in oral health. To address these oral-health disparities, an interdisciplinary team was assembled by a senior faculty member at the School of Dentistry to compete for funding for an Oral Health Center. The Center would carry out several interrelated projects to generate knowledge that would serve to improve the oral health of low-income populations in Detroit. One of the projects was the design of an RCT with two arms. The design of this project was informed by an earlier component, which we refer to as either "the baseline study" or "Phase 1."

The first arm (intervention) of the RCT was a multi-component targeted/tailored motivational interviewing and oral-health education program. The second arm (control) only included an oral-health education component. The main goal of the intervention program was to decrease the rate of caries while improving overall oral health (i.e., brushing and flossing). The design of the intervention was informed by researchers' prior experiences conducting intervention research, their work with disadvantaged populations, and by literature reviews from several fields (i.e., tobacco cessation, mammography screening, physical activity) on the topic of targeting and tailoring to help improve healthier behaviors and reduce less desirable ones. The team focused considerable attention on meta-analyses and systematic reviews and conducted its own systematic review (Bailey, Delva, Gretebeck, Siefert, & Ismail, 2005). The team also obtained extensive baseline data on the constructs that were to be part of the intervention, including detailed information about oral health (i.e., brushing practices); about the availability, accessibility, appropriateness, adequacy, and affordability of dental care; and extensive information about nutritional practices. Also assessed were perceptions, attitudes, and beliefs about oral health, mental health, material hardships, parenting, and numerous other constructs that could serve to inform the intervention (i.e., parent's readiness to change, family and environmental circumstances, experiences of discrimination). Data from the baseline study (Phase 1), described later in this chapter, also were utilized to design the multi-component tailored intervention. Before discussing in detail the sampling and recruitment procedures as well as the implementation of the intervention, we provide important information on the research questions and theoretical model that guided the work.

THE RESEARCH QUESTIONS AND THEORETICAL MODEL

The long-term objective was to develop an effective multi-component tailored/targeted behavioral intervention to promote and maintain good oral health and prevent oral diseases among low-income children and their caregivers. The project sought to assess the effectiveness of the intervention to prevent and reduce gingivitis among caregivers and untreated tooth decay among their children as well as to understand how these clinical outcomes are influenced by personal, environmental, and social factors Participants in the control and intervention groups completed a questionnaire about their oral health and related behaviors and were examined by a dentist. After the dental examination and brief feedback by the dentist, families were stratified according to the caries status of the index child (cavity free, precavities only, cavities) and the child's age. These data were used to randomly assign each child/family into the intervention and control group. We note that some of the text we include in this chapter has been modified from prior work the principal investigator of the intervention project (one of the authors of this book) conducted with the research team for the purpose of developing a *Manual of Procedures* (MOP). As described by the National Institutes of Health (NIH), the purpose of a study MOP is as follows:

> ... [to] facilitate consistency in protocol implementation and data collection across patients and clinical sites. Further, the MOP provides reassurance to all participants that scientific integrity and patient safety are closely monitored and increases the likelihood that the results of the study will be scientifically credible. The MOP is analogous to a toolkit in that it contains information needed for the conduct and operations of a clinical trial. It transforms the study protocol into a guideline that describes the study organization, operational definitions of the data, patient recruitment, screening, enrollment, randomization, and follow-up procedures, data collection methods, data flow, case report forms (CRFs), and quality control procedures. MOP development requires that the final protocol, CRFs, informed consent documents, adverse and serious adverse events reporting, data management, and administrative forms such as Patient Screening Log, Patient Enrollment Log, Delegation of Responsibilities Log, etc., be completed. (http://www.ninds.nih.gov/research/clinical_research/policies/mop.htm. Accessed on January 4, 2009)

Readers who are considering an RCT are encouraged to read in detail the aforementioned NIH site on MOP because it provides considerable detail concerning the type of information that should go into such an important document.

The theoretical framework that guided the work—social cognitive theory (SCT)—was determined through the following systematic process: *(1)* in-depth literature review of educational interventions for similar health behaviors, including mammography screening, prenatal care, and diet; *(2)* review of behavioral theories; and *(3)* analysis of the baseline data to determine relationships among questionnaire items. Based on these findings, SCT guided the tailored/targeted educational intervention that includes an educational video, motivational interviewing, goal setting, resources to overcome social barriers, and follow-up components.

Theories related to behavior change were reviewed in relation to population (low-income African American children and their caregivers), dental behavior, and sensitivity to detect change over time. The theoretical basis for the Education Intervention is SCT (Bandura, 1986). Social cognitive theory was developed from the fields of operant learning, social psychology, and cognitive psychology. The theory postulates that behavior reciprocally influences, and is influenced by, personal as well as social and physical environment factors. In addition, most human behavior is goal directed, purposive, and guided by forethought; therefore, individuals are able to actively shape their environments (Maddux, 1995). As a result, human behavior is based upon behavioral and cognitive sources of influence.

A key personal factor is cognition, which includes perceptions of an individual's confidence (self-efficacy) to perform a behavior. Bandura defines self-efficacy as an expectancy related to an individual's perception of ability to successfully perform an activity or behavior (efficacy expectation) in a particular situation that produces an outcome expectation (given action will lead to a certain outcome). The efficacy expectations can vary in magnitude, generality, and strength. Therefore, the Education Intervention was designed to enhance self-efficacy through promoting successful experiences in meeting realistic goals to attain good oral health.

Based on SCT, the multi-component educational intervention developed includes social, environmental, and cognitive factors to promote an oral-health behavior change that includes brushing teeth, decreasing sugar intake, and visiting a dentist on a regular basis.

LITERATURE REVIEW OF EDUCATIONAL INTERVENTIONS

Several literature reviews were conducted to determine which type of behavior-change interventions and theoretical frameworks were effective for promoting/adopting behaviors, such as mammography screening, prenatal care, and diet. However, we found that limited studies have been conducted for prenatal and diet behaviors which meet the criteria of behavior-change educational interventions conducted in low-income populations. Because there are a large number of studies meeting the criteria for mammography, the literature review focused on mammography screening.

Mammography Screening

The mammography screening systematic review indicated that studies that used peer educators, incorporated multiple intervention strategies, or provided easy access via vans, cost vouchers, or home visits were effective in increasing mammography screenings. However, in our own systematic review we found that mailed letter or telephone reminders were not effective in increasing screening among low-income women (Bailey et al., 2005). Interventions were also evaluated according to the guiding theoretical model, if one was described. These included SLT, the Health Belief Model, the Self-Efficacy Model, the Precede/Proceed Model, the Adherence Model, and the Transtheoretical Model. When studies were grouped by these theoretical models, results were mixed; therefore, use of any particular theoretical model does not imply program efficacy.

Based on the review of theoretical models and behavioral interventions, SCT was selected as the theoretical framework to guide the educational intervention. In particular, the theory postulates that behavior is dependent upon an individual's expectations about the outcomes (positive or negative) of a behavior and the confidence in one's ability to engage in or execute the behavior. This model has been applied to community-based programs such as diet, exercise, mammography screening, and prenatal care. It has also been used for getting rid of negative behaviors such as smoking and drug use. Social cognitive theory has been found to detect changes in behavior over time.

Important social environmental factors of SCT are modeling and social support, which in this study may include access to dental facilities (dental offices) and resources (dentists, finances, transportation) to promote oral health. In addition, in keeping with the tenets of SCT, this intervention was designed to use knowledge and positive reinforcement to improve self-efficacy of oral-health behavior. The knowledge component of the intervention included a video developed for this population. Of note, the dentist in the video was an African American dentist who practices in Detroit. Her patients were African American children residents of the area where the study was underway, and the video was filmed in the neighborhoods from where participants were recruited to participate. All the staff conducting motivational interviewing were African Americans. All the elements of the video and the motivational interviewing component were evaluated and assessed by the scientific and community advisory boards and through feedback we received from additional community members who participated in focus groups. From these meetings, two aspects of the intervention stand out. One is the request by the families not to use rap music as background in the video and that we do not shy away from using medical jargon in any aspect of the intervention. As someone said, "Just because we are poor it doesn't mean we are stupid." Our experience has been that people do not mind if one uses professional jargon or technical terms as long as this information is not communicated with the intention of alienating or creating distance between people. Hence, in our videos, for example, we refer to "caries" as opposed to "cavities" and use other dental and medical jargon that is followed by a friendly explanation. It was also important for families to understand these terms in order to better manage their oral health, particularly to improve their communication with oral-health providers.

Positive reinforcement occurs within the video and motivational interviewing components of the intervention. Confidence in improving oral health (tooth brushing, decreasing sugar intake, and visiting a dentist) was addressed in the video and motivational interviewing. During the motivational interviewing, the participant is encouraged to set realistic oral-health goals that take barriers into account. The participant rates his or her confidence (self-efficacy) to perform the behavior and strategies to overcome the barriers. The purpose of motivational interviewing is to allow for the individual to select the goal he or she wants to work on, rather than having the staff impose a goal on him or her. For this reason, some chose to work on reducing the intake of soda pop at home, not putting children to sleep with a bottle, brushing and flossing at least twice a day after a meal (the most critical time), more assertively communicating with children's daytime caregivers when they insist on giving children high sugary snacks, and working with communities to create community gardens. As the reader can probably see, the tailoring approach taken in this study makes it unnecessary to make broad generalizations about the study population because the information is utilized to be specific to the individual. The educational video used a targeted approach with general oral-health tips that could be helpful to the study populations, while the motivational interviewing component was entirely tailored to individual characteristics. Social and environmental factors (i.e., lack of access to a dentist, ability to pay for care) were addressed through referrals to agencies for access to available community resources. Table 5.1 provides a summary of the various intervention aspects of the study that address the theoretical concepts found in SCT.

Table 5.1 Application of Social Cognitive Theory Concepts to the Intervention

Concept	Definition	Application in Intervention
Environment	Factors that are physically external to the individual	Resources to overcome or cope with social barriers discussed at end of intervention
Behavioral capability	Knowledge and skill to perform the behavior	Mastery of toothbrushing skills through skills training (Video)
Expectations	Anticipated outcomes of the behavior	Modeling of positive outcomes of toothbrushing and decreasing sugar intake via the dentist (Video)
Expectancies	Value that the individual places on the behavior outcome or incentives	Outcomes of good oral health presented in a manner that have functional meaning (Video and MI)
Self-control	Personal regulation of goal-directed behavior or performance	Realistic goals determined by the caregiver

continued

Table 5.1 (Continued)

Observational learning	Behavior that occurs by watching actions and outcomes of other's behaviors	Dentist (credible role model) demonstrated proper toothbrushing
Reinforcements	Responses to an individual's behavior that increase or decrease the likelihood of reoccurrence	Positive reinforcement by the dentist and health advocate; determines incentives rewards
Self-efficacy	An individual's confidence in performing a particular behavior	Behavior change begins in small increments and increases specificity over time
Emotional coping responses	Strategies or tactics used by an individual to deal with emotional stimuli	Problem solving to achieve behavior performance during stressful times
Reciprocal determinism	Dynamic interaction of the person, behavior, and the environment in which the behavior is performed	Intervention includes changing behavior through environmental, skill, and personal change

It is important to note here that while the RCT activities were focused on developing an individually focused intervention, the Oral Health Center had simultaneous additional projects underway. Along with the information obtained from the RCT, and in collaboration with the scientific and community advisory boards, church leaders, and other stakeholders, the Oral Health Center was compiling information for use in lobbying politicians to pass legislation that would serve to improve oral-health care in the City of Detroit and the State of Michigan.

DEVELOPMENT AND IMPLEMENTATION OF THE PROJECT

Sampling and Recruitment

The children were randomly selected from housing units located in the 39 census tracts within Detroit with the highest proportion of

African American households with incomes below 200% of poverty and children under the age of 6 years. The study population consisted of approximately 35,000 households, of which approximately 17% were expected to have eligible children. Families recruited to participate fell in the lowest income areas (less than 250% of the 2000 income poverty line).

Over a period of 3 months, research staff completed a listing of the neighborhoods targeted for the project. The listing process was an identification and documentation of housing units in a designated geographical area. Additionally, the listing process included a listing of all buildings in an area, not just housing units. More specifically, the study sample was selected using a two-stage area probability sample design. In the first stage, 1526 Census blocks in the study area were the primary sampling units. They were listed in Census tract number and block number order. A total of 118 blocks were systematically selected with probability proportionate to size. Some sample blocks contained very few households and posed problems for data collection and statistical estimation. Smaller blocks were linked to larger blocks using an unbiased procedure to obtain sampling units (referred to as "segments") consisting of one or more blocks with a minimum of 100 households. In the second stage, trained study staff went to each of the 118 segments to list all housing units on listing forms. Approximately 14,000 housing units were listed. Businesses and other non-housing units on each block, including empty lots, parks, and other open areas, were also listed. A second stage sample of 12,655 housing units was selected with probabilities inversely proportionate to size. The combination of proportionate to size selection across the two stages yielded an equal chance of selection for all households in the study area (Delva et al., 2005; Delva et al., 2006; Finlayson, Siefert, Ismail, Delva, & Sohn, 2005; Siefert, Finlayson, Williams, Delva, & Ismail, 2007). We note here that in this study, we did not work tacitly with community leaders to gain entry into the communities. However, we did so in an implicit manner in two ways. First, the staff hired to list the properties and to recruit and interview the families were all African American residents of the neighborhoods that were selected to be in the study; hence, the people knocking on doors were neighbors. Second, the site of the project was located in a neighborhood organization, one that provided WIC and other social services, including referrals, to the residents. We rented an entire wing of the building from this organization to set up a dental clinic, lead testing unit, and assessment rooms. Families already were familiar with the organization. We believe this helped build credibility about the study. Furthermore, depending on the families' needs and their interests, staff could immediately walk the person down the hall to the organization's offices for someone there to start the process of assisting the families with issues that may have surfaced during the interview.

Trained interviewing staff visited each sample housing unit. Screening questions were administered at the doorstep to identify households with eligible children, and they listed all eligible children in the household. While data were collected on up to three eligible children per household, one eligible child was randomly chosen for dental examination. The recruitment process located and scheduled around 1400 families. Of those 1021 visited the Dental Assessment Center (DAC) and completed the examinations and interviews (Phase 1). The average income of the families was less than $10,000; 40% of caregivers were smokers; and the majority of the caregivers did not complete high school education. Building support of the community for the project took several years. The project had a Community and a Scientific Advisory Committee. The project also raised funds from foundations and other sources to pay for the dental care of the recruited families.

The interview and examinations conducted at the DAC focused on assessing the association between tooth decay levels in children and their caregivers; the social, behavioral, and biological (lead toxicity) risk factors; access to health care; and quality of life at the home and community. The data that were collected during this baseline stage of this project (Phase 1) served to assist in answering the following question:

> Why are some low-income African-American children disease free and others not, even when they live in or experience similar social, behavioral, economic, and neighborhood environments?

Development of Educational Intervention

In this baseline stage (Phase 1), 27 statements addressing oral-health beliefs were presented, and participants were asked to respond to them.

Examples of these statements are as follows: "Most children eventually develop dental caries," "There is not much I can do to stop my child from developing dental cavities," "There is nothing wrong with putting a baby to bed with a bottle," and "Cavities in baby teeth don't matter since they fall out anyway." Findings from the analyses of these data, which compared beliefs and attitudes as a function of the index child's caries levels, were utilized to inform which beliefs and attitudes would be selected to be targets of the intervention. Not only were statistical differences considered, but discussions also took place to consider the clinical (dental) significance of these beliefs and attitudes in relation to oral health. We used the participants' own responses and the dentists' assessments to guide our intervention. In this sense, the intervention could not get any more specific or tailored, and hence sensitive, to the individual child's circumstances. Whether some of these responses may be considered a cultural element of low-income African Americans living in Detroit is an empirical question. In this study, our intention was not to search for cultural elements to make sweeping generalizations about the larger African American community. Rather, our intention was to design an intervention that was sensitive to the family's and child's circumstances and to implement an intervention tailored to the individual child's and mother's characteristics. We are now in the process of evaluating the effectiveness of the intervention.

Development of an Oral-Health Video

Development of a video was informed by the theoretical framework, results of the oral-health belief items conducted in the Phase 1 data analyses, and focus groups conducted at the DAC. The video was developed to address the targeted oral-health beliefs, good oral-health practices, and barriers in achieving good oral-health practices. The video starts with an explanation of teeth and the process of tooth decay. Next is a section showing and describing how to brush children's teeth at various age levels, and then the video describes how eating habits affect the process of tooth decay. Throughout the video there are messages which address oral-health beliefs (determined by the results in Phase 1) and barriers in achieving good oral-health practices (determined in community focus groups).

The video explains the following: the relationship between sugary and starchy foods and the caries process, the benefits of drinking Detroit's fluoridated water, details about cariogenic effects of sugary drinks, how to read labels on food packages, the appropriate amount of daily sugar intake, the benefits of using a cup instead of a bottle, healthy food and drink alternatives, and tips on how to help children eat healthier. In the video, messages relating to oral-health beliefs were intertwined within the oral-health education messages. Positive messages addressing these beliefs were purposely placed throughout the video. Examples of the messages include the following: pre-cavities can be stopped, fluoride in the tap water and toothpaste make teeth strong and heal pre-cavities, you can help your child be cavity free, baby teeth are important, cavities can be prevented, and you can prevent your child from developing cavities.

Focus groups with community residents were held to determine barriers of brushing children's teeth. Some of the barriers that were reported during these groups included the following:

- Being too busy
- Forgetting
- Being too tired
- Too much to do being a single parent
- Child forgets
- Parent does not have good brushing habits, so it is hard to enforce good habits on child laziness
- No energy

During the focus group, participants also raised the issue of the difficulty in controlling what children eat. Anyone, and particularly any parent of young children, can probably relate to the above barriers and the challenges below. Comments included the following:

- Children eat too much candy, juices, and cereals.
- Sugary snacks are cheaper than fresh fruit.
- Children beg for candy until the parent gives in.
- Candy makes the children quiet for awhile.
- When children visit friends or relatives, they eat anything they want without limits.

The video addressed some of the barriers by addressing the following:

- How to engage children in brushing
- How to involve toys in the brushing process
- How to make brushing fun
- Establishing a brushing routine
- Brushing together
- Brushing at the time of day when the person has the most energy
- Praising children when they brush their teeth
- Giving children hugs
- Interacting with them as a reward

To address eating habits, the video delivered the following messages: give your children foods that are lower in sugar, like fresh fruits, fresh vegetable, dried fruits, yogurt or cheese; give your children canned fruits that do not have sugar added; give your children water or water mixed with unsweetened fruit juice; teach your children to make healthier choices when away from home; and praise your children when they make good choices.

Motivational Interviewing

Motivational interviewing (MI) is a counseling style that arose from the field of alcoholism (Miller, 1983). The purpose of this approach is to work on minimizing the natural resistance that individuals tend to experience when their beliefs and behaviors are challenged (e.g., a person with a diagnosis of alcohol dependence having to make a decision to discontinue drinking). Motivational interviewing is a directive, client-centered counseling approach intended to help clients explore and resolve ambivalence they may experience when faced with the choice of making lifestyle changes (Rollnick & Miller, 1995). Persons conducting MI are trained to communicate in an empathic, direct, and supportive manner in order to minimize normal resistance. The "best" environment for MI to take place is one that is supportive, nonjudgmental, and that conveys to people that they are perfectly capable of making changes. The nonjudgmental attitude, in turn, permits people to safely explore new behaviors.

Motivational interviewing has often been implemented within the context of the "stage of change" or "transtheoretical model" (TTM)

(Prochaska & DiClemente , 1983). According to TTM, a person may fall within any one of five stages, often drifting back and forth between stages. The first defined stage is the *precontemplation stage*, where a person is not yet thinking in serious terms about making any changes in the next 6 months. The next stage is the *contemplation stage*, where a person begins to think seriously about behavioral changes within the next 6 months. The next stage, *preparation stage*, refers to a stage whereby a person is prepared to take action and intends to make a change within, for example, the next 30 days. This person also may suggest that in the past 6 months she or he has tried making changes. The next stage, the *action stage* refers to a person who has made a change within the last 6 months. And finally, the *maintenance stage* is applied to a person who has maintained a behavior change for longer than 6 months. Reliance on MI ensured that our intervention was tailored to the specific characteristics of each individual and family and not some stereotypical consideration of the population—an approach that is consistent with the intersectionality perspective we present in Chapter 7.

Results from the first year of data collection (Phase 1) and from focus groups, however, indicated that most caregivers reported being in the action or maintenance stage of tooth brushing, either with their own teeth or their children's teeth. It became clear that it was not socially appropriate for respondents to share less than proper dental hygiene. Therefore, a decision was made by the research team to implement MI without TTM. Quite interestingly, when MI principles are followed, the person's readiness for change is automatically taken into consideration. This situation results from the individualized approach that MI elicits. That is, in using MI, the health advocate does not impose her or his values and goals on the caregiver but is still able to assist the participant in exploring ways to improve the child's oral health according to the parent's willingness and ability to move toward the adoption of healthier behaviors that will lead to improved oral health.

A helpful framework under which MI was implemented is given by the acronym FRAMES, which stands for giving *f*eedback, getting the person to take *r*esponsibility for the change that needs to take place, providing brief *a*dvice, helping the person create a *m*enu of options, using *e*mpathy throughout the interaction, and assisting the person to build her or his *s*elf-efficacy to accomplish the goals they defined jointly with the health advocate.

Goal Setting

Self-reinforcement through goal setting and problem solving enhances the effectiveness of participants to integrate effective oral-health practices into their daily lives.

Rationale for Screening and Referral for Social/Environmental Barriers

The decision to screen caregivers for potential barriers to maintaining or improving their children's oral health was informed by the PRECEDE portion of the Precede-Proceed model for health education planning (Green & Kreuter, 2005), as well as by the Phase 1 survey findings and the information obtained from focus groups and other key informants. The Precede-Proceed model is a robust and well-tested ecological approach to health promotion and health education that posits that the environment influences the individual behavior that occurs in it, and that changing environmental factors can modify health behavior. PRECEDE stands for predisposing, reinforcing, and enabling factors in educational/environmental diagnosis and evaluation. Consistent with the project's social cognitive theoretical framework, this planning model groups predisposing factors: knowledge, attitudes, beliefs, values, and perceptions; reinforcing factors, or the rewards the caregiver receives from accomplishing her oral-health goals; and enabling factors: the skills, resources, or barriers that can enhance or inhibit a caregiver's success in accomplishing her or his goals. By identifying the presence or absence of enabling factors, particularly those related to material hardship and chronic stress, and by providing the caregiver with referrals to those resources needed to overcome social and environmental barriers to behavioral change, we aim to maximize her likelihood of success.

Randomization

Prior to randomization, the 1021 index children were stratified by age and caries prevalence assessed in Phase 1 (sound, early carious lesions only, cavitated carious lesions). The assignment of the children was masked (concealed) from the participants, research team, DAC staff (except staff at the coordination desk and MI health advocate), and examining dentists, and it was kept with the Center's director until after the data were analyzed in subsequent years.

Masking and Unmasking

In this trial, and given the nature of the intervention and flow of families at the DAC, it would not be possible to maintain full concealment of group assignment. Concealment, however, was maintained from the data analysts, project principal investigator, and staff who were not directly related to educational intervention (coordination desk, MI health advocate, and control intervention staff), and from the examining dentist. The group to which each child was assigned was delivered to the coordination desk in a sealed envelope, which contained an assignment sheet listing the name of the child and the caregiver, as well as the identification numbers. Once a child completed the dental examination, the envelope was opened and the group assignment was shared with the dental educator assigned to either the multi-component or standard oral-health education (control) groups. The child's chart only indicated whether the child was assigned to group 1 or 2. We next briefly describe the components of the intervention group followed by a description of the control group's activities. We conclude the section with some information about the consent process.

INTERVENTION GROUP: MULTI-COMPONENT TAILORED/TARGETED MOTIVATIONAL INTERVIEWING AND VIDEO ON ORAL-HEALTH INTERVENTION

All of the preliminary work described earlier resulted in the development and implementation of five intervention components. The staff hired to implement the intervention were called "health advocates" rather than "educators" because an advocate represents someone willing to not simply educate the caregiver but also to advocate for services and to serve as a partner in enhancing oral health with the caregivers and their children. All health advocates were African American women. All of the staff were African Americans, and all were residents of the City of Detroit. The five components of the intervention are summarized here:

1. First, the counseling strategy (MI) was utilized to guide how health advocates would establish rapport with the caregiver, review the results of the dental examination, provide caregivers with feedback, and would begin the discussion with the caregiver of goals that will lead to enhanced oral health for her children and herself.

2. Second, caregivers were shown a 15-minute oral-health video designed specifically to address the beliefs, attitudes, and behaviors of the population under investigation. The video was informed by the results of the data analyses from Phase 1 as well as from the feedback received from more than a dozen focus groups conducted. The health advocate encouraged caregivers to do tailored stops of the video. This means that the caregiver is not a passive receiver of information.

3. Third, after discussing the video and the information presented concerning the dental assessments and parenting/psychosocial questionnaires, the health advocate encouraged the caregiver to think about what she would like her children and her own oral health to be like in the future. These steps lead the caregiver to define feasible and measurable goals that would be used to improve her child's and family's oral health. A discussion ensued of the type of behavioral barriers (e.g., barriers directly related to the behavior, such as caregiver working late into the night, which make it more difficult to supervise tooth brushing of her child at night) and material hardship barriers (e.g., unemployment) that might make it more difficult to adopt a new behavior to improve oral health. Identifying ways to address these barriers was an important job of the health advocate. Through this process of personalized goal setting and identification of steps to overcome barriers, health advocates helped caregivers enhance the self-efficacy concerning her belief that she can improve the child's oral health.

4. Fourth, after the goals were well defined, the health advocate would review the caregivers' list of things that might get in the way. This overview permitted the health advocate to ask the caregiver if she wanted assistance with a referral to an agency to receive help with any of these problems. A referral mechanism was in place to assist caregivers. This component was in place because a large number of the study participants faced severe material hardships, including unemployment, water, heat, and food shortages, as well as chronic

stressors such as infants and children being bitten by rats. It was hypothesized that by attending to these needs, the effectiveness of the oral-health intervention we designed will be strengthened. Unfortunately, a serious structural problem consisted of the overall lack of services available in the city for these families. The dental project was physically located in the building that housed the Neighborhood Services Organization (NSO), a human services agency that provided a range of social and employment services to the local community. Space was rented from the NSO for two reasons. First, it provided the team with an immediate setting (literally down the hallway) to help families connect with necessary services. Second, in this manner the project could contribute financially by helping the NSO defray costs of using the building they inhabited.

5. The fifth and final component consisted of conducting two to three follow-up boosters beginning at 2 weeks after implementation of the intervention. The follow-up boosters consisted of tailored mailed family and child-oriented reminders and telephone calls. The purpose of the follow-up boosters is twofold. One purpose of the follow-up boosters served to remind the caregiver about the goals they set out to accomplish and to help them brainstorm solutions to barriers that may have arisen in their attempts to implement the goals. A second purpose was for tracking. Continuous follow-up permitted tracking of participants to minimize attrition. In addition, families were sent free toothbrushes and toothpaste.

CONTROL GROUP: VIDEO ON ORAL-HEALTH EDUCATION INTERVENTION

Caregivers randomly assigned to the Video on Oral-Health Education Intervention Group received the equivalent of Components II, IV, and V from the Multi-Component Tailored/Targeted Intervention group, described earlier. The main differences were as follows: (a) caregivers watched the educational video but unlike those in the Multi-Component Tailored/Targeted Intervention group the health advocate left the room, participants were not prompted to stop the video to discuss its content, and once the video was shown they were asked if they had any questions. If they had none, they were led to the next activity; *(b)* caregivers were told that there was a list of agencies that they might want to contact in the future in case they need assistance with different life stressors. The agency list was then given to the caregiver. At the same time, the research staff asked the caregiver if she would like to meet with an intake counselor at the NSO; and *(c)* follow-up intervals were the same but these were not designed as "boosters." Unlike the personalized information provided to participants in the Multi-Component Tailored/Targeted Intervention group, the follow-ups in the control group consisted of sending generalized oral-health tips. The families in the control group also received free toothpaste and toothbrushes every 3 months.

The above activities reflected the research team's decision to offer participants in the control group more information than the "usual care package." A usual care set of activities may have been to provide families with the results of the dental assessments and some handouts with general information about good oral practice. However, given the known information about good oral health, it was decided for ethical concerns that individuals in the control group should also be exposed to the oral-health video that was specifically designed with information from the baseline survey and that included content that was entirely pertinent to low-income residents living in Detroit. The selection of the material to be presented to the control group (more information than usual care) is an example of the team's desire to be sensitive to the population's life circumstances. The difference between the two RCT arms would be the manner by which the research staff would engage with the families. Essentially, the research staff would not engage in MI with participants in the control group. Before concluding this chapter, we briefly describe below the consent process undertaken in this study.

INFORMED CONSENT PROCESS

All participating families filled out the appropriate consent forms before they completed interviews, a dental examination, height and weight measurement, and blood and saliva sample collection (adults only) at the DAC. These data were used to develop the intervention arms of the RCT. For the RCT, the study families were invited to return to the DAC to repeat interviews, a dental examination, height and weight measurement, and blood sample collection (children only).

Upon arrival of each family to the DAC, the research staff at the Exit/Entry desk would complete the necessary check for identifications (for caregiver and the index child). Each family (adult caregiver) was asked to sign on consent forms for this phase of the project. A copy of the consent form was given to the participant and it was read aloud. Research staff were trained to be certain that the respondent is fully informed about the study and the rights and responsibilities of participating. Once the consent form was read, the research staff asked the respondent for additional questions. Then, she was asked to sign two copies of the form. A copy was kept by the research team and a second copy given to the caregiver. The following consents were obtained from study participants:

- *Consent form for participation in the Detroit Dental Health Project.* This is the primary consent for caregivers to participate in the project.
- *HIPAA: authorization for use and disclosure of protected health information.* This consent was utilized in order to allow the project to have access to all the information collected at the DAC.
- *Declaration regarding caregiving or legal guardianship.* This form was utilized to certify the individual's caregiving/legal guardianship status to the child as the person who could provide consent for the child to be examined for signs of tooth decay.
- *Consent form for a waiver to access to the Medicaid record,* This consent was obtained in order to allow the research team to have access to the child's Medicaid treatment records, if he or she participates or has participated in the Medicaid program. The purpose is to review the child's dental treatment records from Medicaid to monitor dental treatments, dental health status, and treatment needs.
- *Assent for minor participants.* This assent consisted of a brief and child-appropriate explanation of the dental exam and height and weight collection read to the child by a dentist or other staff person at the DAC.
- *Permission for child(ren) to stay in supervised play area.* This consent requested parental consent for children to be supervised by a project staff member in the play area.

- *Consent form for participants in the focus groups.* This consent was obtained from focus group participants.
- *Consent form for participants for audio/videotape recording.* This consent was used to permit the project staff to audio or videotape the interview for quality assurance process.

Because there were no serious risks involved in the educational intervention and evaluation process, the NIH/NIDCR did not require this project to establish a formal data safety monitoring board (DSMB). A DSMB is part of a system for the oversight and monitoring of clinical trials in order to ensure participants' safety and data integrity. Instead, the data safety and monitoring activity of this project team included close monitoring of intervention and data collection at the DAC, tracking for quality assurance, and regular reporting to the management committee and the NIH officer.

CONCLUSION

In this chapter, we provide considerable detail of the comprehensive amount of work that was done to conceptualize a two-armed RCT to design and test a tailored intervention and to select the best theoretical framework to guide it. In fact, because much of the literature on behavior change focused on white middle-upper class individuals, we conducted our own systematic review focusing on lower-income populations and racial/ethnic minority populations. As is usually the case, once we focused our work on these populations, the findings differed from those obtained with non-Hispanic white populations. These findings reinforced the need to be very careful to generalize findings obtained from general populations to racial/ethnic and low-income populations and therefore the need to conduct more investigations with diverse groups. However, in our own study we also are very cautious about generalizing the findings of the present study to other African American communities, those living in different regions, in rural areas, and those of middle and upper socioeconomic status, among others.

As we repeatedly mentioned throughout the chapter, the tailoring approach, guided by motivational interviewing, meant that the intervention was extremely specific to the individual and the family characteristics. In this study, we were looking for information to tailor the intervention. This makes for a very powerful intervention approach—one that takes whatever identities and contexts are important to that individual (and in this case, the family) into consideration. For all parents the intervention involved dealing with specific oral-health practices, but this was tailored based on the result of their dental assessment and answers to the questionnaires. For some parents the intervention involved focusing on economic challenges and the challenges of raising children, though the nature of these varied considerably between families. For some parents the intervention focused on dealing with mental-health problems they may be experiencing, for some it involved dealing with relationship issues, and for others it involved finding care or receiving quality care. Tailoring allowed us to take all of these differences into consideration when discussing ways to improve their and their children's oral health. In other words, sensitivity to the population meant that *all* the work was tailored to match the needs and context of low-income African American residents of Detroit. We also had, and continue to have, numerous activities underway that target politicians to address structural issues low-income individuals face when seeking oral-health care.

In this chapter we also provide a description of the phases that preceded the implementation of the RCT. Unlike the first three chapters, in this chapter we did not focus on data-analytic approaches, though we do make some comments about this task. Phase 1 involved drawing a large representative sample of residents who met the study's inclusion criteria by using complex sampling techniques, focus groups, and interviews with residents. We also obtained baseline data from the participants themselves. All of these pieces of information played an important role in the design and implementation of the RCT.

This chapter provides considerable detail about the process and activities involved in the implementation of a two-armed RCT that we hope readers will find useful when considering their own studies. The number of RCT variations that one can implement is vast (Campbell & Stanley, 1966). Even though we report what may be the simplest type (a two-armed RCT design), nothing about the study was simple.

6

Conducting Community-Based Participatory Research

This chapter describes the implementation of a community-based participatory research (CBPR) project, a partnership approach to research in which academic, community-based and community serving organizations, and residents equally share expertise and responsibility for planning, conducting, evaluating, and disseminating the results of the research. Knowledge and products gained from the research are directed to improving community well-being. Examples are drawn from the Good Neighborhoods community change process led and funded by the Skillman Foundation. In addition to describing what guided the formulation of the research question(s), the theoretical model, and the development and implementation of the project, we will also discuss the following topics: How does community-based research differ from other approaches? What are the epistemological, methodological, and institutional issues arising from community partners, faculty members, and students? Why is community-based research an important approach for achieving social work objectives? How is it congruent with the values of the profession?

DEFINITION OF COMMUNITY-BASED PARTICIPATORY RESEARCH

Community-based participatory research (CBPR) is a collaborative approach to research that seeks to equitably involve all partners in the research process and recognizes the unique strengths that each brings to the process. Community-based participatory research begins with a research topic of importance to the community with the aim of combining knowledge and action for social change (Minkler & Wallenstein, 2003). Most CBPR falls on a continuum of how involved the community is with the research and researcher, but it all aims to eliminate the "laboratory" perception of the community being investigated (Green et al., 1995). This continuum, conceptualized with two dimensions, is based on the answers to two questions: *(1)* Who directly controls the decision making? *(2)* Who actively conducts the research activities (Hick, 1997)

DEFINITION OF COMMUNITY

The definition of community may be based on one of two factors: geographical location (e.g., a neighborhood) or functional commonality (e.g., a common identity, a common interest, a common problem, or a similar demographic). The key to defining community for the purposes of collaborative relationships is ensuring that the people who are most interested and affected by the partnership are being included in the decision making and/or set the priorities for the research.

THE HISTORY OF COMMUNITY-BASED PARTICIPATORY RESEARCH

Community-based participatory research can trace its roots to the action research of Kurt Lewin (1946) through the social justice movement of the 1970s, where it was used to mobilize (Friere, 1970) research marginalized communities (Hall, Gillete, & Tandon, 1982). More recently, CBPR has played a role in the field of public health, where it has evolved into a popular paradigm and is now gaining momentum in the field of social work. The premise of the CBPR approach is congruent in many ways with the values and respective missions of the profession of social work, some of which are as follows:

1. Recognition of the worth and dignity of each human being
2. The right to self-determination or self-realization
3. Respect for individual potential and support for an individual's aspirations to attain it
4. The right for each individual to be different from one another and be accorded respect for those differences (Bartlette, 1970)

Within the social work discipline, community organization became a separate emphasis for training in the 1950s, and it reached its peak enrollment in social work programs during the 1960s and 1970s. During that era, emphasis was placed on differentiating community organization from other forms of social work practice and to define the practice models associated with community organization (Rothman & Epstein, 1977). It is this foundation of community practice that CBPR builds upon.

In social work, the community is widely accepted as one possible unit of analysis along with individuals, groups of individuals, and systems within the community (e.g., schools, government, and churches). Community-based participatory research is congruent with these values because it emphasizes and encourages the input of all individuals in the community and seeks to bring these vested parties together to promote social change guided by common understanding, interests, and input.

The core value of self-determination is inherent in CBPR. Community members have information to share about the issues they are facing, as well as ideas about how to solve them. Their participation in the identification of issues and suggestions for resolution/intervention are steps in the empowerment process.

GUIDING PRINCIPLES OF COMMUNITY-BASED PARTICIPATORY RESEARCH

The key elements of the CBPR approach are presented below, but this is by no means a static list. The principles of CBPR are integrated from several fields, and they should continue to grow and evolve through research and evaluation of new projects and techniques.

- Community-based participatory research is a collaborative relationship between the academy and the community.
- Community-based participatory research must involve the community, both the people affected by the research topic and those who are not affected. This allows for opposing viewpoints to be considered. Community members become nontraditional students.
- The community should help define the issues/goals of the research. Community concerns drive the research questions. This is the inverse of what typically happens in the university, where researchers routinely form the questions and in some instances community priorities are ignored.
- The community, and the research partners therein, are involved in decision making at all phases of the research, including data collection, interpretation of results, and the application of those results to address community concerns (Israel, Schulz, Parker, & Becker, 1998).
- The research builds on the strengths of the community, including resources, and relationships. This would include social capital (Allen-Meares, 2008), as well as physical resources, and the skills and knowledge of individuals in the community.
- The research is linked to education of the community and informed action by the community, meaning that findings and knowledge gained are disseminated to all partners in the research. The ultimate objective of CBPR is social action that leads to social change that leads to social justice.
- Informed action by the community creates new networks that endure past the end of the research project. All partners are considered experts with complementary knowledge and skills (Macaulay et al., 1998), as well as co-learners—the community learning about research, and researchers learning more about context and social problems.

While these guiding principles are the basis for effective CBPR, Jacobson and Rugele (2007) outlined other principles that should be at the forefront of any CBPR project:

- *Engaging with questions of power, difference, and inequality.* Because CBPR in social work has a social justice component, it is necessary for these questions to be addressed in the planning phase of the project. These questions include the following: How can power be discussed? How can a climate be established that values all partners' contributions?

- *Identifying and reducing barriers to people's participation.*[1] This is a corollary to the principles already discussed because it is necessary for community participation as partners in the research regardless of topic. These barriers can occur on personal, institutional, political, economic, and cultural levels (Beresford & Hoban, 2005).

- *Creating an inclusive space for teaching-learning.* Teaching-learning emphasizes the dialogue, collaboration, and mutuality of the assessment phase of the change process (Finn & Jacobson, 2003).

- *Establishing an environment of mutual support and expectation.* Conceptualizing a CBPR project as a mutual aid system and a basis for collective support and action locates all participants— including the social worker—as learners, teachers, facilitators, and actors. Group members share data, engage in the dialectical process, explore taboo subjects, experience the "all in the same boat" phenomenon, help each other with specific problems, and feel the power of "strength in numbers" (Shulman, 2006, pp. 269–278).

- *Making connections among the personal, political, cultural, and historical.* Group members tend to connect their personal troubles to powerful social, political, and economic systems, and they reevaluate their tendency to internalize society's messages that simplify problems to individual failings alone (Jacobson & Rugele, 2007).

- *Building knowledge from people's lived experiences.* Those who bear the greatest burden of unsustainable policies ought to have the loudest voice in the policy-making process (Beresford & Hoban, 2005).

- *Taking action and accompanying the process.* With the social worker inside the process, he or she is accompanying the process of change, not simply monitoring the work done by the group members (Jacobson & Rugele, 2007).

- *Evaluation, critical reflection, and celebration.* Evaluation answers questions about whether the actions taken have been congruent with the values of social justice. Critical reflection requires open-mindedness, responsibility, and wholeheartedness (Dewey, 1933). Celebration is rarely discussed or considered a core process in U.S. social work practice, but it is essential for "embracing the rewarding, difficult, uplifting, disappointing, and energizing efforts of social justice-oriented group work" (Jacobson & Rugele, 2007, p. 33).

Methodology

Community-based participatory research runs the gamut of methodological perspectives. As in all social science research, the specific methods are driven by the research question and population. In most cases, the community collaboration is somewhat standardized. The research begins with assessment of need in a particular community. This can be accomplished through community survey and focus groups as in Kim et al.'s (2008) ongoing community involvement, or via the case of the Urban Research Centers studied by Israel et al. (2006). Assessment may also begin with the recognition of a community issue through the independent study of a researcher (Gittelsohn et al., 2008), or as a response to a widespread problem in a particular geographic area (i.e., poverty, homelessness).

Community-based participatory research can employ a diverse range of study designs and methods. Examples include environmental assessments, randomized controlled trials, Photovoice, and qualitative case studies. Kim et al. (2006) use a quasi-experimental, delayed intervention design with differing levels of assignment and observation. This approach allowed them to access the social capital of each assignment group while assessing the intervention at the individual level. Gittelsohn et al. (2008), in their study of the activity levels of adolescent girls, used a combination of quantitative and qualitative methods in a randomized field trial of interventions. The lack of standardization across centers is the biggest concern of a field trial of this sort, and it can be addressed by the theory that is driving the research (Gittelsohn et al., 2008).

Community-based participatory research is untraditional in its methodology. Some critics believe its results may lack objectivity, reliability, and generalization. Furthermore, the partners in CBPR have the power to change the focus, methods, and outcomes of the research. Critics argue that this could compromise the results. Regardless of the specific methodology used, the merits of which can be judged by the accepted standards of that methodology, some emphasis must be placed on the value of knowledge translation, and the cultural and social validity to assess the research relevance and community engagement in the research (Cargo & Mercer, 2008).

Some of the methodological issues that can arise with CBPR are a lack of evidence that interventions truly contributed to positive change; the inability to specify fully all aspects of the research up front; not finding an acceptable balance between research and action; meeting various time demands that would allow all partners to be actively involved in the research process; and the challenge of interpreting and integrating data from multiple sources. The first mitigating factor of these issues is, in fact, the very flexibility of the methodology that some may criticize. Other facilitating factors include the involvement of community members in research activities (i.e., training community members to conduct research interviews), which enhances the quality of the process and the results; an ongoing analysis of the community's strengths, resources, structure, and dynamics, which enhances the relevance and appropriateness of all aspects of the research and intervention; and the joint agreement by all partners on the research principles, which can specify the parameters around issues such as confidentiality and access to data.

IMPLEMENTATION

As in all research, there are a number of potential challenges when creating academic and community partnerships: lack of trust; inequitable sharing of power and control; conflicts with differences in perspective, priorities, assumptions, values, beliefs, and language; conflicts over funding (i.e., Who is the fiduciary of the funds? How are they distributed? What amounts are provided to different partners?); conflicts based on the emphasis on task versus process; conflicts arising because of the time-consuming process (to establish and maintain trusting relationships); and conflicts over the definition of community. General challenges for the partnerships include competing institutional demands. Because most institutions of higher education place value on traditional research approaches and federal funding, some researchers may risk securing tenure or attaining a promotion due to the time spent on building relationships and developing trust. In addition to the other procedural demands of CBPR, the time spent on these activities can delay the rate of publications, for instance.

David Fasenfest and Larry Gant (2005) offer a few additional challenges of traditional CBPR:

1. *Lack of trust and respect.* After so many years of being probed and provided with little to show for their efforts, it is understandable that the next time a university knocks at the door the community can be hesitant to answer.

2. *Inequitable distribution of power.* Are "equal" partnerships truly equal?

3. *Conflicts and differences in perspective.* The university may differ on what is most important and/or what are reasonable outcomes for the community to achieve. Conflicts associated with differences in values, beliefs, and language are typical.

4. *Time.* An investment of time is required to create true partnerships and to engage in community–based research (e.g., time to build relationships, time for faculty involvement, time needed to process respective approaches, time to handle unforeseen challenges). For example, working with the Hmong population required taking the time to develop a positive relationship with a Hmong community elder. Once this individual was "in," access to the Hmong community flowed.

5. *Conflict over financial resources.* Who holds the bank account? Who is the principal investigator of the grant? How are these decisions made?

6. *Conflicts associated with different emphases on task and process.* The university partner may be more interested in completing the project and all relevant tasks required by the funding agents, whereas the community might be more interested in the process—being inclusive, hearing the many voices, and building the spirit of cohesiveness.

7. *Who represents the community and how the community is defined.* Who is excluded? Who solves disputes if issues surface? Who speaks for the community?

8. *Sustainability after the project ends.* When the grant or interest in the research project ends, how does one prevent the community from feeling used/exploited? Many communities seek long-term commitment or sustainability over time. We all know that faculty interests evolve over time and that funding sources are finite. The institutionalization of a structure to facilitate CBPR has been the solution to address these issues.

9. *The faculty reward system.* In some institutions, the faculty reward system may work against CBPR: the time needed to build partnerships with the community can take considerable effort, thus taking attention away from academic tasks such as writing for publications. Junior faculty members that are heavily involved in long-term CBPR projects such as Good Neighborhoods may be unable to publish results from the project as early as they would like (Shanks, 2008).

10. *Simultaneous research.* Multiple researchers trying to work in the same community can be confusing for community members and messy for evaluation because multiple approaches are being implemented or studied at the same time (Shanks, 2008).

BENEFITS

Although there are challenges to building a successful and positive CBPR relationship, there are benefits as well. Community-based participatory research has various benefits for the university and the community. From the community, the university receives knowledge and information to contextualize the research. The research also provides a wonderful learning experience for the students who are involved in the project. By stepping into the community, both faculty and students experience a worldview and perspective other than their own, which can enhance understanding (Maurrasse, 2001, p.123).

Similarly, the community can mobilize its resources to facilitate the objectives of the project. Community members can draw upon new resources, such as university staff, materials, and experts, and in some cases additional financial resources are available. Community members can often find empowerment through CBPR because they learn new skills and enhance their ability to problem solve through participation in the process. The community also receives acknowledgment that it too has resources, experiences, and unique contributions to the partnership. In other words, the expertise of the community is acknowledged and leveraged for the project's successful outcome (Allen-Meares, 2008). The community can also "hook in" to the university's credibility as a consequence of the partnership.

Additional facilitating factors for the partnerships include the following: jointly developing norms; identifying common goals and objectives; democratic leadership; presence of community organizer; involvement of support staff/team; researcher's role, skills, and competencies; prior history of positive working relationships; and identification of key community members. General facilitating factors for the partnerships include broad-based support, top down and bottom up; provision of incentives (both financial and abstract, see benefits); and actions promoting policy changes (i.e., changing standards for Tenure and Promotion because of CBPR).

GOOD NEIGHBORHOODS: AN EXAMPLE

For 45 years the Skillman Foundation's strategy for improving the well-being of children in metro Detroit has been to define community problems, then make grants to organizations that have the ability, expertise, and resources to address them. "The Good Neighborhoods Initiative (GNI) is a very different model," says Carol Goss, the foundation's president and chief executive officer. The new program actively engages neighborhood residents to prioritize their needs and develop action plans in an effort to create environments where children can thrive. It is an 8- to 10-year initiative. (Freligh, 2006)

Prospectively funded for 10 years (2005–2015) by the Skillman Foundation (Detroit, Michigan), six neighborhoods in Detroit (Chadsey/Condon, Vernor, Brightmoor, Cody/Rouge, Osborn, and Central/Northern) were identified based on a variety of demographic factors and assessments. Good Neighborhoods seeks to develop place-based strategies that will result in enhanced social, health, education, and employment outcomes and declines in problematic youth indicators (e.g. health disparities, excess mortality, teen pregnancy, delinquency, high school dropout rates) for children and youth in Detroit. The expectations are captured in a tagline for Good Neighborhoods: "To change the odds for children and youth in Detroit." In 2005, the Skillman Foundation funded the Principle Investigator at the University of Michigan School of Social Work to provide technical assistance for Good Neighborhoods and she invited key faculty at the UM-SSW to work with her, providing strategic information, research competencies, and resources to support the goals, activities, and outcomes of the initiative.

Encouraged by positive outcomes in other large urban centers, Skillman committed to a 10-year initiative in hopes of demonstrating enough author change to attract larger funders. With the principle investigator and her team, Skillman found a resource for research, policy briefs, concept papers, and problem solving, and together they developed the Technical Assistance Center (TAC) to meet Skillman's needs and locate the foci of their efforts. Key faculty involved in the project have research knowledge of community-based research methods, evaluation, community organizing and development, poverty, empowerment, and race/ethnicity (Gant, 2008).

Skillman chose six Detroit neighborhoods as project participants based on their large numbers of children, multiple needs, and community readiness to address problems. During the initial 2-year phase, the technical assistance focused on helping these communities' residents study and shape their distinct priorities and corresponding neighborhood action plans by convening focus groups, providing data about their neighborhoods, increasing their capacity to develop priorities based on data, and developing strategic outcome-focused action plans to address their community needs.

In addition to faculty, as many as 60 University of Michigan students participate as part of a class. The class meets in Detroit in the heart of the city as a base for university–city collaborations. The class blends theory and practice and provides a platform for in-depth student participation in Good Neighborhoods.

The initiative kicked off January 28, 2006, with a community meeting, one in a series of gatherings scheduled to take place in all six neighborhoods, facilitated by representatives of Skillman and the TAC.

Early turnout was encouraging, attracting in some cases more than 300 people at some meetings, with the dialogue facilitated by University of Michigan faculty. In the first year, community participants, National Community Development Institute (NCDI), and University of Michigan social work students and faculty identified priorities and formulated plans to improve children's lives.

In the second year, the Principle Investigator and select members of the faculty at the UM-SSW provided technical assistance to the neighborhood action teams as they began to implement their action plans. With various degrees of comfort and experience with actuating plans, the university helped develop appropriate workshops and curricula for residents to learn how to monitor their action plans independently. Skillman asked the University of Michigan students of social work and the NCDI to develop a leadership academy to enable residents to lead and sustain development change in their neighborhoods (Gant, 2008).

During the remaining years, the foundation hopes to see neighborhoods create a governance structure to turn plans into reality and to evaluate outcomes. Early and enthusiastic data collection/employment efforts such as the use of Photovoice (to be discussed more fully later in this chapter) by community youth will become the springboard for activism and empowerment in the future. This early project demonstrated the ability of the tri-partite partnership to effect change, employ youth, and animate activism within the community.

THEORY OF CHANGE

As a consequence of numerous community focus groups and meetings (see Fig. 6.1) held in the selected six communities, the University of Michigan Skillman team developed its theory of change (see Fig. 6.2). Please note that the theory of change recognized the critical players and the interaction among them, as well as the desired outcomes and indicators of success for key activities (see Fig. 6.3) or the logic model. The community change process has been very organic (meaning that the change process has been driven by the community members at the grassroots level). The theory of change is based on the belief that the residents of the Good Neighborhoods have many assets and skills to bring about the changes they desire and the ability to assist with data

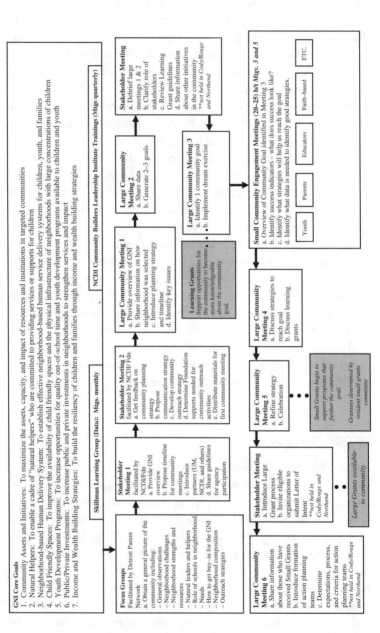

Figure 6.1 Planning phase I: community goal and strategy areas. (From Ziedens & McGee, 2006.)

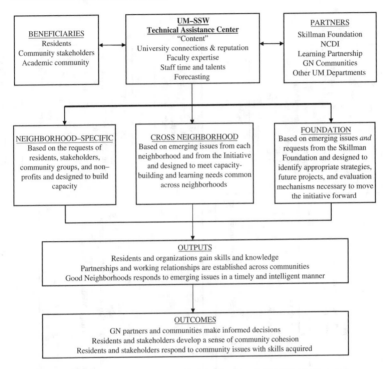

Figure 6.2 Theory of change. GN, Good Neighborhood; NCDI, National Community Development Institute. (From Allen-Meares et al., 2008.)

collection to determine success. By sharing information and receiving new knowledge, residents can build upon their strengths and work together to renew their neighborhoods.

The team also developed a multi-level technical assistance strategy (see Fig. 6.4) with the ultimate objectives being to create partnerships among all stakeholders to share knowledge, and optimize communication, so that community capacity was enhanced to promote the well-being of children. As each community articulated its specific objectives, interventions were discussed and approaches to the evaluation of outcomes were defined and implemented. Some of the strategies used to assess outcomes included contextualized evaluation, reflection surveys, and skill assessment charts. In other words, data sources were triangulated.

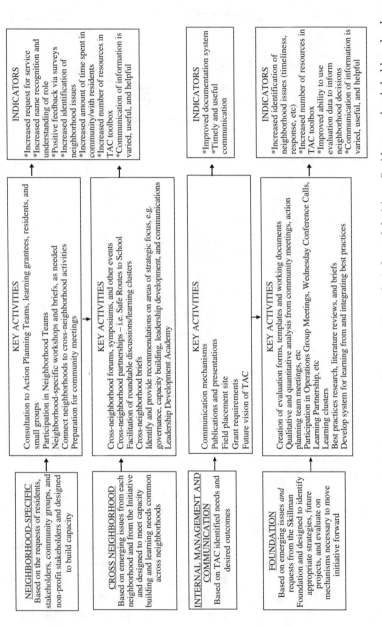

Figure 6.3 Outcomes: Good Neighborhood partners and communities make informed decisions. Residents and stakeholders develop a sense of community cohesion (Prepared by the TAC).

Cross-Neighborhood Technical Assistance	Neighborhood Specific Technical Assistance	Technical Assistance to the overall GNI
Cross-neighborhood Technical Assistance deals with technical assistance that relates to more than a single, specific GNI neighborhood. Cross-neighborhood technical assistance serves to meet the capacity-building and learning needs that are common across GNI neighborhoods, and once met, will move the initiative forward at the neighborhood level: This type of technical assistance may be determined by identifying common themes through (qualitative) analysis contained in a variety of documents, such as: GNI Learning Grants, Large Community meeting notes, Action Planning Team meeting notes, and/or Action Plans. This type of technical assistance may be provided through: • Workshops • Technical Assistance Briefs • Small Roundtable Discussions • Brown bag lunches • Meetings and would be open to residents/stakeholders/partners from all GNI neighborhoods.	Neighborhood Specific Technical Assistance is based on specific requests for technical assistance from neighborhood residents, stakeholders, community groups, non-profit organizations engaged with the GNI. Neighborhood specific technical assistance serves to meet the capacity-building needs at the individual neighborhood level. This type of technical assistance is often solicited through requests from individual residents, community groups, or non-profit organizations, or at the recommendation of the initiative. This type of technical assistance is most often provided in the following manner: • Individual consultation with residents, community groups, or non-profits. • Producing the data reports for Phase I large community meetings (#1-3) in collaboration with others. • Participation on the Community Teams • Technical assistance briefs	Technical Assistance to the overall Good Neighborhoods Initiative serves to meet the capacity-building needs related to determining appropriate strategies, future projects, evaluation mechanisms necessary to move the entire initiative forward in a deliberate, intentional manner. ***Also includes…Technical Assistance requested by Skillman Foundation*** Technical Assistance requested by the Skillman Foundation includes Foundation requests for data/information/reports for a variety of purposes. This type of technical assistance generally entails producing • Reports (Qualitative analysis) • Technical assistance briefs • Binders of relevant information • Evaluations (Quantitative analysis) • Templates/working documents • Literature reviews • Operations team meetings • Weekly conference calls • Learning partnership meetings

Five Areas for Technical Assistance: These areas for technical assistance, identified by the Skillman Foundation in June 2006, cut across all levels of TA (above).

1. Governance: What are key questions/issues? *Examples:* How will the Initiative be governed in each community? What should the governance structure look like? What are additional considerations?	2. Partnerships: What are key questions/issues? *Examples:* What partnerships need to be present? Who should be collaborating? (Policy change & grassroots)? Who are intermediaries?	3. Communication: What are key questions/issues? *Examples:* How should communication be handled in the Initiative? What are tools? (Think with and across communities)	4. Leadership Development: What are key questions/issues? *Examples:* What leadership development models would be helpful to the GNI communities?

5. Capacity Building: What are key questions/issues? *Examples:* What capacities should be built in each neighborhood? What capacities do we need to develop to implement the Initiative? (Relates to 1-4 above, as well as multi-level TA strategy.)

Figure 6.4 Multi-level technical assistance strategy. GNI, Good Neighborhoods Initiative; TA, technical assistance. (From Ziedens & McGee, 2007.)

The Good Neighborhoods Initiative includes numerous intervention projects such as a youth crime prevention, leadership academy, and Photovoice, among others. For illustration purposes, we next describe the development and implementation of the Photovoice project because it illustrates a powerful method to engage youth in community participatory research.

GOOD NEIGHBORHOODS INTERVENTIONS: PHOTOVOICE IN DETROIT

Photovoice is the process of putting cameras into the hands of community members (whether geographical or social identity community members) to allow them to become recorders and potential catalysts for social change (Goodhart et al., 2006). Through this process it is expected that Photovoice becomes a social justice advocacy technique that empowers individuals to create change within their community (Molloy, 2007). Caroline Wang and Mary Ann Burris (1997), the two founders of Photovoice, state that there are three main goals of Photovoice: *(1)* to enable people to record and reflect their community's strengths and concerns, *(2)* to promote critical dialogue and knowledge about important issue through large and small group discussion of photographs, and *(3)* to reach policy makers.

Photovoice was based on the Freirian Theory of Critical Consciousness (Wang & Burris, 1997), in which individuals are encouraged to analyze the problems that they often see within their lives and dialogue about these issues. Feminist theory and practice may have also influenced Photovoice, with the recognition that there is a male bias that has influenced participatory research (Wang & Burris, 1997).

Photovoice has been used throughout the world to empower individuals who have historically not been given a voice in the communities in which they live. Photovoice was first used among the village women in Yuman Province, China (Wang, Morrel-Samuels, Hutchison, Bell, & Pestronk, 2004), and it has also been used extensively throughout the United States. For instance, Photovoice has given the youth and adults of Flint, Michigan, a chance to participate in a community-building exercise and explain their frustrations and hopes as residents of their city. Additionally, Photovoice was used in after-school activities programs for youth in Baltimore, Maryland, which allowed them to demonstrate the ways their community needed further support (Strack, Magill, & McDonagh, 2004). Photovoice has even been used to empower elementary school students in Contra Costa, California (Wilson et al., 2007). All of these projects have been highly successful in engaging the residents of the selected communities in the Photovoice project and allowing them to have a voice and create social change within their communities.

The Good Neighborhoods project has been quite successful in mobilizing adults, but far less so in mobilizing youth. While all six Good Neighborhoods have generated action plans for community development and empowerment, youth in five neighborhoods literally had no systematic or organized voice in developing or responding to these action plans. This has resulted in poor youth attendance and participation in the planning processes for these five neighborhoods.

As a result of a recent presentation at the American Evaluation Association conference on the use of Photovoice in community development initiatives (Love & Muggah, 2005), Foundation staff became interested in using Photovoice as a youth mobilization strategy. Following this interest, project staff were trained in the use of Photovoice as a community intervention and agreed to deploy—and assess—a Photovoice intervention (See Allen-Meares et al., 2008 for the discussion of Photovoice contained on this page through page 134).

Approximately six to eight youth and School of Social Work interns were hired in each community to work with university staff to capture photographically their perceptions of the community themes and change objectives represented by their neighborhood action-planning teams. All youth were trained in the approach, and consent for participation was obtained. Photovoice data analysis and discussion forms were created, as was a participation evaluation form.

The implementation of Photovoice requires the development of themes that define the boundaries for the particular social advocacy project or initiative. Skillman and TAC determined that efficient boundaries for the current deployment of Photovoice for youth in the five communities would be the action plan short- and long-term priorities as well as any implementation strategies or activities generated. The following simple example illustrates this.

Crime and Safety Action Plan

Long-term priority—A: youth crime prevention. To foster a proactive
environment that will encourage, support, and develop youth to
become more productive through positive activities that will
improve their quality of life.
Short-term priority—A: youth crime prevention. Enroll youth and
families in specified programming.
Implementation strategy—A: youth crime prevention. Conduct
inventory to determine current successful and underutilized
programs as well as document gaps and identify partners to provide
resources.

Using a popular education (Frierian) approach, the Photovoice facilitators engaged the youth in strategic discussion about the action plan and
what it meant for them as young people (e.g., the meaning of crime prevention for youth, what programming might be needed, and what their role in
prevention would be (beyond that of service recipient or client). The
discussion would then turn to examples of pictures that reflect youth
thoughts or positions on crime prevention. Youth then reduce the number
of photos to a critical few, using an iterative process called SHOWED. Youth
examine each photograph through the lens of six questions:

1. What do you see here?
2. What's really happening here?
3. How does this relate to our lives?
4. Why does this problem/condition exist?
5. How could this image educate the community/policy makers?
6. What can we do about it (the problem/condition)?

Deployment of Photovoice requires a public presentation and discussion of photographs in a public community space, and a final creation of an action plan and agenda by participants. The participating
students in the Skillman project ($n = 60$; about 13 per each neighborhood) were instructed by University of Michigan School of Art staff in
photo design and displays, creating fixed and movable art presentations
for exhibition at the University of Michigan Detroit Center at Orchestra
Place (each lasting 2 weeks) with rotation out to permanent locations in

the five participating Good Neighborhoods. Each neighborhood had an opening night reception facilitated by the student photographers and hosted by the University of Michigan Schools of Art and Social Work. At this reception, students' neighborhood-focused action plans were presented.

The resulting critical dialogues allowed youth to showcase their work and share their stories, thoughts, hopes, and dreams for the community with each attendee. The outcome of these events was powerful. Two community exhibitions have been moved into neighborhood settings. One community exhibition was showcased at a trustee meeting of The Skillman Foundation. Michigan's Children, a statewide child advocacy organization, is now interested in helping the youth present the exhibit to the state legislature. Coverage of the Photovoice exhibitions and an article about the project was published in a local weekly newspaper, *The Metro Times*.

By stimulating critical dialogue of the issues raised in the photographs, Photovoice participants generated awareness not just of problems or concerns but also of potential solutions and areas of strength with respect to their lives and communities. The images and stories can be shared with an audience in numerous ways, including presentations, exhibits, books, videos, CD-ROM, and the Internet.

RESEARCH DESIGN OF THE PHOTOVOICE PROJECT

The research design is a validation substudy for a much larger initiative to be deployed within 1–3 years from the present date. The current validation substudy reflects a pre-experimental pre-post design deployed with a small sample ($n = 60$) of youth aged 13–18 years residing in one of the six Good Neighborhoods. Typically, attrition is not an issue with Photovoice interventions due to the brevity and interest in the activities. Nonetheless, we expect attrition of about 10% and will conduct the intervention without replacement. As the first cohort of Photovoice youth was being recruited, the staff proposed that a testable hypothesis be formed and tested via the collection of pre- and post-data using a standardized survey of student engagement (National Survey of Student Engagement, 2008). This was the first step in examining the empirical contributions of possible evidence-based effects of Photovoice. Further, the specific aims of this project were identified as follows:

1. The examination of the associations between youth participation in an intervention and changes in attitudes and behavior in involvement in neighborhood community development initiatives.

   a. Hypothesis 1: Compared to baseline, youth will report more positive attitudes and beliefs about youth-related service or civic engagement.
   b. Hypothesis 2: Compared to baseline, participating youth will report greater intention to engage in specific community service activities associated with Good Neighborhoods.
   c. Hypothesis 3: Compared to baseline, participating youth will report greater active involvement with specific community service activities associated with Good Neighborhoods.
   d. Hypothesis 4: Compared to baseline, participating youth will report greater active involvement with community service activities external to Good Neighborhoods.

Participant Activities

Students participated as follows:

1. Completion of baseline and post-test surveys
2. Photovoice training
3. Photography in community
4. Interpretation of photographs
5. Mounting of photographs at gallery space (Detroit Center at Orchestra Place)
6. Community reception of Photovoice projects
7. Relocation of Photovoice projects for permanent displays in each neighborhood

Measures

Quantitative

Youth completed baseline and post-test measures, for example, demographics incorporated within the larger National Survey of Student

Engagement (NSSE, 2008). The NSSE obtains, on an annual basis, information from hundreds of 4-year colleges and universities nationwide about student participation in programs and activities that institutions provide for their learning and personal development. The results provide an estimate of how undergraduates spend their time and what they gain from attending college. Survey items on The National Survey of Student Engagement represent empirically confirmed "good practices" in undergraduate education. That is, they reflect behaviors by students and institutions that are associated with desired outcomes of college. While typically used for first-year college students, NSSE has been used by high schools interested in assessing service learning environments for high school students (NSSE, 2008).

Qualitative

The Photovoice process resulted in provision of tangible documents (photos plus written commentary by photographers). It is possible that some of these documents and comments may be used as examples and evidence of students' changes in service-related attitudes or intentions in related publications or articles. Student identities remained anonymous or identified by alpha numerics in any presentation.

Analyses

The common analysis of Photovoice data is qualitative (content/thematic analysis). Rarely are additional (quantitative) measures of youth engagement/leadership used in related analysis. Our quantitative analysis of Photovoice does not address the content of the photos or narrative write-ups of the youth. Instead, it frames Photovoice as an intervention that (hopefully) impacts student perceptions of youth engagement—hence the tests on the pre-post measures of youth engagement. Subsequently, we are following the typical presentation of univariate and cross-tabular presentations of demographic information, utilizing demographics as covariates as needed in our comparative t-tests between pre-posttest scores. The analysis will be largely exploratory in function because we have not hypothesized differences in outcome by age cohort, gender, or other demographic characteristics. The small sample size encourages some conservatism in inferences made and analyses attempted; the study is somewhat underpowered unless we assume substantial intervention effect of the Photovoice project itself, and there is no empirical support to warrant this assumption.

Facilitators

Photovoice facilitators are five graduate students of social work who served as interns. All graduate students have been trained in Photovoice instruction by the principal investigators. One student developed the training manual used as the basis for instruction. Each graduate student led the Photovoice initiative in one of the five neighborhoods selected (Vernon neighborhood declined participation due to intensive use of Photovoice in youth work previous to this intervention). Students have developed timetables in conjunction with Good Neighborhoods Community Liaisons in each neighborhood.

Recruitment

Students have developed unique recruitment venues and strategies reflecting available resources in each neighborhood. Consistent across each neighborhood is identification of an informational meeting discussing Photovoice, including eligibility, completion of consent forms for parents and assent forms for youth under 18 years of age, and stipend payment (incentives). In each community, community liaisons and staff supplement general recruitment efforts with identification of specific groups of youth who may have been involved or a participant in any previous Good Neighborhood meetings or planning sessions.

Incentives

Youth can receive up to $500 for participation in the Photovoice Project. Incentives are operationalized as hourly work for students (approximately $12/hr) and include hours in training, photography, analysis, narrative reflections, and display setup.

CONCLUSION

In this chapter we provide a rich description of the history of CBPR. An invaluable collaborative approach to the potpourri of methodologies that bridge the academy and the community, CBPR is a participatory process in which co-learning and capacity building take place. It is an empowering process that achieves a balance between research and action, and it can contribute to translational/contextualized science (Minkler & Wallenstein, 2003).

The use of Photovoice is an exciting example of innovative strategies that can be identified and implemented from the partnerships that exists among community residents, academics, and funding sources to further engage residents and to reach out to those less likely to be active (youth), in order to have their voices heard and to influence their communities in a positive way.

In fact, the GNI considers the implementation of Photovoice a successful part of the overall project. Although there have been challenges, the youth and their communities have experienced positive change via their participation. The ultimate challenge is building on this momentum as the project goes forward.

The faculty and staff members have identified their own suggestions for success as they view their roles in CBPR. In closing, and based on these experiences, we list the following suggestions to consider for others participating in this method of community change:

1. Create a common language that allows for effective and respectful communication while recognizing the adult literacy level of the neighborhood and participants. This involves a lot of dialogue (Gant, 2008; Miller, 2008). Flowcharts that detail timelines and expectations allow all stakeholders to understand roles and to have a big picture perspective of the process (Gant, 2008).
2. Create an "operations committee" responsible for logistics and strategic planning between the key stakeholders (Gant, 2008).
3. Hold frequent meetings to help facilitate dialogue and cement relationships. The three major stakeholders of the Good Neighborhoods project meet weekly (as possible) for an hour or more, with good results (Gant, 2008).

4. Foster good communication among the senior leadership. They need to communicate well, particularly to discuss broad issues of trust, how to facilitate discussion across cultures, and the different ways of working that collide with an enterprise like Good Neighborhoods (Gant, 2008).

7

Discussion

In this pocket series book, we describe the culturally appropriate implementation of various methods that social work researchers and those in allied disciplines may utilize to conduct research. Some rely on a more emic perspective, others take an etic approach, and yet others utilize a combination of these. We acknowledge, however, that the approach we have taken may not match the traditional approach taken by cross-cultural researchers, who look for cultural elements unique to a particular population and who may tend to make broad generalizations about the populations they study. As we state in the introductory chapter, we purposely decided to offer readers an approach to conduct research, one that emphasized being sensitive to the individual without relying on broad statements about groups. We believe this "tailoring" approach is more informative than one that relies on overly broad and potentially inaccurate generalizations about people that take on essentialist (i.e., static or unchanging) characteristics. We prefer our approach because our main concern is about being sensitive to the particular population we work with, regardless of whether sensitivity takes a cultural, gender, racial/ethnic, intergenerational, or socioeconomic lens. In writing this book, we recognize that our tendency to examine multiple identities, as opposed to what may be only cultural elements, stems from the fact that most of our projects were conducted in urban areas with populations with a more cosmopolitan than traditional way of life. Indeed, the reader will notice that most of the more salient statements we make about cultural elements are found in Chapter 2, where we describe the projects with American Indians who live on rural reservations.

For this book we specifically selected examples of mixed-methods, population-based survey, longitudinal, experimental design (a two-armed randomized clinical trial), and community-based participatory research methods because these are some of the most frequently utilized approaches to answer research questions commonly studied by social workers and other professionals. These five research methods do not cover the entire gamut of designs available to study research questions because this would be impossible to do in one book. Hence, the selection of these five particular methods was influenced by our intimate knowledge of these designs as applied to the diverse population groups we have worked with. We strongly felt that in describing these projects and their application with the populations we have worked with, we could offer insights that otherwise would not have been possible had we not led these studies. Thus, intimate knowledge of the projects allowed us to provide rich descriptions.

As indicated in the introductory section, in selecting these topics we neglected others. For example, we do not cover a number of important research designs (e.g., ethnographic research, quasi-experimental designs, case studies, case-control studies, cross-over designs), innovative data collection strategies (i.e., Ecological Momentary Assessments), and populations (e.g., a particular Latino, Asian American, Pacific Islander, or Arab population living in the United States or other countries). We obviously do not have the expertise to discuss all the research designs, innovative data collection methods, and population groups, nor would one book provide the space needed to accomplish such a gargantuan task. As a matter of fact, it was quite difficult to narrow down and select the topics we wanted to discuss for each project because *all* play an important role in the successful implementation of a project. In the end, the selection of research methods, populations, and projects reflects our professional and personal interests.

In that spirit, each chapter presents a rich description of selected aspects of each project as applied to a diverse population. Despite the differences in research methods and populations, several threads connect them. One of the most salient is the importance of developing partnerships among people—a theme that connects all the research designs and projects presented here. Some of these partnerships are between researchers with different training, research foci, and paradigms. Other partnerships are between researchers and study participants. No matter what the research design and population studied, we feel strongly about creating partnerships with researchers of different disciplinary orientations and conducting research *with* and not *on* people.

We also emphasize throughout the chapters that high-quality relationships take time to develop and to maintain. This is another common thread: these collaborations do not surface overnight and that they must be nurtured. To create trusting relationships it is important for people to invest considerable time and effort. How exactly these relationship are created may vary from population to population, but what does not vary is the willingness of all parties involved, and particularly researchers, to listen and respect each others' perspectives. We say "particularly researchers" because of the inherent hierarchical structures generated by those with academic training and those without. From our point of view, respecting each others' perspectives does not mean that all ideas proposed will be implemented. Rather, it means a willingness to respect the different ways of knowing and sharing information, to actively invite different opinions and perspectives, and to seriously consider them before making a decision about the research step that will be taken—a decision that is guided by the particular research question(s). A researcher who invites diverse opinions but then makes decisions unilaterally and ignores these other points of view is not what we have in mind when we speak of collaboration.

Another thread is the careful attention paid to the protection of human subjects throughout the research process. We are honored that people whom we may have never met before have trusted us and opened their doors to share parts of their lives with us. In doing so, they have opened their lives to the rest of the world as a result of the publications, reports, and presentations researchers may produce. As such, we want to make sure their rights and privacy are fully protected. Protecting study participants is an activity that we take very seriously. In our respective projects we have done everything possible to minimize the potential harms that may result from their voluntary participation in our study.

A final thread is that all of the projects described in this book received some form of funding, some of it quite substantial. We highlight this point because it provides additional evidence that one need not conduct research on a shoestring budget, a point emphasized by Delva and Castillo (in press) when discussing international collaborations but that also applies to domestic research. As we write this discussion, we realize we do not describe the extent to which personal funds were utilized to build collaborations (i.e., mileage, travel expenses, numerous meals, phone calls, use of volunteers) and to what extent these costs were (or were not often times) covered by university (course releases) and pilot funds (small internal grants). It is expected that investing personal resources into these partnerships is a necessary activity and one that we do not hesitate using even if reimbursement is not possible. Nonetheless, creating research teams that can enhance one's chances of being competitive in order to receive adequate funding to carry out a study, we suggest, should be a realistic goal of one's research agenda. Resources are needed to tackle complex problems because these require more complex approaches that only the availability of additional resources can facilitate.

WHAT IS NEXT IN CROSS-CULTURAL RESEARCH: INCORPORATING AN INTERSECTIONALITY LENS

Our experiences conducting cross-cultural research lead us to posit that cross-cultural researchers will need to pay increased attention to the concept of intersectionality as espoused by feminist thought and research, and by the growing theoretical and empirical literature on gender and sexual identity (Cole, 2009; Diamond & Butterworth, 2008; Shields, 2008). We make this suggestion because we find that with the increased interconnectedness of peoples around the world—of worldviews, beliefs, attitudes, and behaviors (traditional and modern), intertwined with various other identities (i.e., gender and sexual identities, race and ethnicity, socioeconomic position)—that cultural elements are becoming more fluid, changing, and dynamic. They are increasingly more difficult to distinguish or separate from these other identities, assuming that it is even possible to do so. Because the focus of this book is on cross-cultural research, throughout this book we encourage cross-cultural researchers to consider these other identities when conducting their work. However, the reverse is true as well. Research on gender and sexual identity, socioeconomic position, and other identities, will be strengthened if that work on intersectionality paid greater attention to cultural elements and to racial and ethnic differences.

Before we conclude, we offer the following statements that we aspire toward in our own work, not just to be sensitive to cultures but also to other identities, so that individuals and families can fit outside the box:

- Consider cultural elements as fluid and dynamic that are multiply determined and that occur within a geopolitical and historical context.
- Consider other identities, such as immigration status, generational status, cohort, sex, gender and sexual identities, wealth, income, educational level, occupational status, race and ethnicity, among others, before making statements about culture.
- Consider that observed behaviors, values, beliefs, and attitudes have a distribution within a population and that these intersect and overlap in multiple and complex ways with the distributions of the above identities.
- Measuring and making statements about the specific behaviors, values, beliefs, and attitudes are more important goals than coming up with a buzz or catch-all word to capture this complexity.
- Consider research questions that are more focused on understanding associations, interrelationships, or variations between constructs and their corresponding variables than on estimating an average of a variable for the specific purpose of making a sweeping statement about the population under investigation. Essentially, aim more to explain than to describe.
- Avoid making gross generalizations.
- Show respect by validating peoples' experiences through the art of active listening, making a sincere effort to understand differences and communicating in a respectful manner.
- Identify the gatekeepers and invite them to be partners or collaborators. Study and learn the customs and languages of the populations you work with. Do not simply rely on hiring people from these groups as staff. Live and share experiences with them so that you can learn *from* them.

In conclusion, we sincerely hope that readers can benefit from the experiences we describe in this book and can adapt at least some of these to their own work. We consider ourselves privileged to be able to present examples of work done in countries other than the United States. Whether the work is done in the United States or in another country, the same threads described earlier apply. In closing, we would appreciate hearing your thoughts about what we have written so that we may further improve our work. We certainly would very much enjoy discussing research ideas you may have. This would facilitate our learning and may even result in exciting collaborations.

Glossary

Community-based participatory research (CBPR) A collaborative approach to research that seeks to equitably involve all partners in the research process and recognizes the unique strengths that each brings to the process.

Cross-cultural research A natural experiment involving cultural groups in which the researcher is interested in existing relationships among variables under circumstances where these variables have been modified by cultural conditions.

Cultural sensitivity A continuing, incessant, and open-ended series of substantive and methodological insertions and adaptations designed to mesh the process of inquiry with the ethno-cultural characteristics of the group being studied.

Emergent design Allows for subsequent steps or procedures in the research process, including the research questions, to evolve or change from the input of the study participants.

Emic Approach in which the culture is studied from within, with constructs specific to that culture.

Epistemology The branch of philosophy that studies the nature of knowledge, its presuppositions and foundations, and its extent and validity.

Essentialist models Refers to a model or a perspective of culture, gender, race/ethnicity, etc. that defines these elements as having fixed, static, or unchanging characteristics.

Etic Approach in which the culture is studied from without and compared across cultures to identify universal constructs.

Etiology Used to refer to the causes or origin of disease, such as the factors that produce or predispose toward a certain disease or disorder.

Focus groups Carefully planned series of discussions designed to obtain perceptions on adefined area of interest in a permissive, nonthreatening environment (Krueger & Casey, 2000).

Gatekeeping role Refers to the formal or informal process set up by individuals, families, communities, groups, or countries to allow "outsiders" (i.e., researchers) access to their lives.

Indian reservation A piece of land in the United States designated as federal territory and managed by an American Indian tribal council. The reservation is under the jurisdiction of the U.S. Department of the Interior's Bureau of Indian Affairs. Many reservations are not the ancestral land of the tribe that inhabits them because Indians were forcibly moved to undesirable lands. The name "reservation" comes from the conception of the Indian tribes as independent sovereign nations when the U.S. Constitution was ratified. In the treaties with Indians, the tribes gave up large portions of land to the United States and designated parcels that the tribes "reserved" for themselves. Those parcels came to be called "reservations."

Institutional Review Board (IRB) A committee that has been formally designated to approve, monitor, and review biomedical and behavioral research involving humans with the aim to protect the rights and welfare of the research subjects.

Longitudinal studies A correlational research study that involves studying the same group of individuals over an extended period of time.

Methodological In this book the term is used broadly to refer to research design and statistical topics.

Mixed-methods research The collection, analyses, and integration of quantitative and qualitative data in a single study or in multiple studies in a sustained program of inquiry.

National Academy of Sciences (NAS) An honorific society of distinguished scholars engaged in scientific and engineering research, dedicated to the furtherance of science and technology and to their use for the general welfare.

National Institutes of Health (NIH) A part of the U.S. Department of Health and Human Services; the primary federal agency for conducting and supporting medical research.

Randomized clinical trial (RCT) A study in which participants are assigned randomly (by chance alone) to different treatments or conditions.

Statistical power The probability that the test will reject a false null hypothesis (a hypothesis that states there is no difference).

Talking circles A traditional form of group communication among Indian people. An object, usually an eagle feather or a shell, is passed around to each person to hold when he or she is speaking. Every person has an opportunity to talk. People who are talking are not interrupted, and they can talk as long as they want.

Tribal chief Usually the head of the tribe or clan. However, tribal chiefs do not necessarily have to be the head or tribal chairman of a tribe. Sometimes a chief is a distinguished and respected elder of the tribe who has gained this status by his actions and oftentimes his way of living and acting in a traditional way.

Tribal council A tribe's legislative body, which is comprised of tribal members who are elected by eligible tribal voters. In some tribes, the council is comprised of all eligible adult tribal members. Although some tribes require a referendum by their members to enact laws, a tribal council generally acts as any other legislative body in creating laws, authorizing expenditures, appropriating funds, and conducting oversight of activities carried out by the chief executive and tribal government employees. An elected tribal council and chief executive, recognized as such by the Secretary of the Interior, have authority to speak and act for the tribe as a whole, and to represent it in negotiations with federal, state, and local governments.

Tribal member Defined differently for different tribal groups. Tribal constitutions set forth membership criteria. Usually lineal descendancy from someone on the tribe's enrollment list or from someone who may have been an original allotee when land was allotted to the tribe is a requirements for membership/ enrollment. Other tribes use blood quantum, tribal residency, or continued contact with the tribe.

Notes

CHAPTER 1

1. National Academy of Sciences, National Academy of Engineering, and Institute of Medicine. (2005). *Facilitating interdisciplinary research*. Washington, DC: National Academies Press. Available online at http://www.nap.edu.

CHAPTER 4

1. For more information on the potential mechanisms linking ecological stress and compromised immune systems, the reader is encouraged to read the articles by Aiello, Simanek, & Galea, 2008; Dowd, Aiello, & Alley, 2008; Dowd, Haan, Moore, Blythe, & Aiello, 2008; and Zajacova, Dowd, & Aiello,2009.

CHAPTER 6

1. Sherry Arnstein's (1969) classic social participation ladder suggests many types of participation. Only a few of these are transformative, and many of them reinforce inequities and social hierarchies.

References

Aiello, A. E., Simanek, A., & Galea, S. (2008). Population levels of psychological stress, herpesvirus reactivation and HIV. *AIDS and Behavior.* DOI: 10.1007/s10461-008-9358-4.

Allen-Meares, P. (2008). Schools of social work contribution to community partnership: The renewal of the social compact in higher education. *Journal of Human Behavior in Social Environment, 18*(2), 77–100.

Allen-Meares, P., Gant, L., Hollingsworth, L., Shanks, T., McGee, K., Miller, P., & Williams, R. (2008). *Theory of change.* University of Michigan, School of Social Work, Technical Assistance Center. Unpublished report.

Ambler, M. (1995). History in the first person: Always valued in the Native world, oral history gains respect among western scholars. *Tribal College Journal of American Indian Higher Education, 6*(4), 4–11.

Aguinis, H., & Henle, C. A. (2001). Empirical assessment of the ethics of the Bogus Pipeline. *Journal of Applied Social Psychology, 31*, 352–375.

Anthony, J. C. (2002). Epidemiology of drug dependence. In K. L. Davis, D. Charney, J. T. Coyle, & C. Nemeroff (Eds.), *Neuropsychopharmacology: The fifth generation of progress* (pp. 1557–1573). Philadelphia: Lippincott Williams & Wilkins.

Anthony, J. C., & Van Etten, M. L. (1998). Epidemiology and its rubrics. In A. Bellack & M. Hersen (Eds.), *Comprehensive clinical psychology* (pp. 355–390). Oxford, England: Elsevier Science Publications.

Arnstein, S. R. (1969). A ladder of citizen participation. *Journal of the American Institute of Planners, 35*(4), 216–224.

Attneave, C. (1969). Therapy in tribal settings and urban network intervention. *Family Process, 8*, 192–210.

Autti-Ramo, I. (2000). Twelve-year follow-up of children exposed to alcohol in utero. *Developmental Medicine and Child Neurology, 42*, 406–411.

Bailey, T., Delva, J., Gretebeck, K., Siefert, K., & Ismail, A. (2005). A systematic review of mammography educational interventions for low-income populations. *American Journal of Health Promotion, 20,* 96–105.

Bandura, A. (1986). *Social foundations of thought and action: A social cognitive theory.* Englewood Cliffs, NJ: Prentice Hall.

Bartlette, H. M. (1970). *The common base of social work practice.* Washington, DC: National Association of Social Workers.

Becker, S. A., Affonso, D. D., & Blue Horse Beard, M. (2006). Talking Circles: Northern Plains Tribe's American Indian women's views of cancer as a health issue. *Public Health Nursing, 23*(1), 27–36.

Ben-Shlomo, Y., & Kuh, D. (2002). A life course approach to chronic disease epidemiology: conceptual models, empirical challenges and interdisciplinary perspectives. *International Journal of Epidemiology, 31,* 285–293.

Beresford, P., & Hoban, M. (2005). *Participation in anti-poverty and regeneration work and research: Overcoming barriers and creating opportunities.* New York: Joseph Rowntree Foundation.

Blanchard, E. L., & Barsh, R. L. (1980). What is best for tribal children? A response to Fischler. *Social Work, 25,* 350–357.

Boyatzis, R. E. (1998). *Transforming qualitative information: Thematic analysis and code development.* Thousand Oaks, CA: Sage Publications.

Brislin, R. W. (1983). Cross-cultural research in psychology. *Annual Review of Psychology, 34,* 363–400.

Bronfenbrenner, U. & Ceci, S. J. (1994). Nature-nurture reconceptualized in developmental perspective: A bioecological model. *Psychological Review, 101,* 568–586.

Caldwell, J. Y., Davis, J. D., DuBois, B., Echo-Hawk, H., Erickson, J.S., Goin, R. T., et al. (2005). Culturally competent research with American Indians and Alaska Natives: Findings and recommendations of the first symposium of the work group on American Indian research and program evaluation methodology. *American Indian and Alaska Native Mental Health Research: The Journal of the National Center, 12*(1), 1–21.

Campbell, D. T., & Stanley, J. (1966). *Experimental and quasi-experimental designs for research.* Chicago: R. McNally.

Canino, G., Lewis-Fernandez, R., & Bravo, M. (1997). Methodological challenges in cross-cultural mental health research. *Transcultural Psychiatry, 34,* 163–184.

Cargo, M., & Mercer, S. L. (2008). The value and challenges of participatory research: Strengthening its practice. *Annual Review Public Health, 29,* 325–350.

Caris, L. (1992, December). *Drug surveillance system in Central America, Panama, and the Dominican Republic: OAS/CICAD PAHO Project first results.* Report presented at the Community Epidemiology Workgroup (CEWG).

Chen, C-Y., Dormitzer, C. M., Bejarano, J., & Anthony, J. C. (2004). Religiosity and the earliest stages of adolescent drug involvement in seven countries of Latin America. *American Journal of Epidemiology, 159,* 1180–1188.

Cochran, W. G. (1977). *Sampling techniques* (3rd ed.). New York: John Wiley & Sons.

Cohen, J. (1988). *Statistical power analysis for the behavioral sciences* (2nd ed.). Hillsdale, NJ: Erlbaum.

Cone, E. J. (1997). New developments in biological measures of drug prevalence. In L. Harrison & A. Hughes (Eds.), *The validity of self-reported drug use: Improving the accuracy of survey estimates* (National Institute on Drug Abuse Research Monograph Series #167, pp. 108–129). Rockville, MD: U.S. Department of Health and Human Services.

Cook, T. D., & Campbell, D. T. (1979). *Quasi-experimentation: Design and analysis issues for field settings.* Boston: Houghton-Mifflin.

Costello, J. E., Compton, S. N., Keeler, G., & Angold, A. (2003). Relationships between poverty and psychopathology: A natural experiment. *Journal of the American Medical Association, 290*(15), 2023–2029.

Cozzetto, D. A., & Larocque, B. W. (1996). Compulsive gambling in the Indian community: A North Dakota case study. *American Indian Culture and Research Journal, 20*(1), 73–86.

Crazy Bull, C. (1997). A Native conversation about research and scholarship. *Tribal College Journal of American Indian Higher Education, 9*(1), 17–23.

Creswell, J. W. (2003). *Research design: Qualitative, quantitative, and mixed methods approaches* (2nd ed.). Thousand Oaks, CA: Sage Publications.

Davis, S., & Reid, R. (1999). Practicing participatory research in American Indian communities. *American Journal of Clinical Nutrition, 69*(4), 755–759.

De Jong, M. D., Galasso, G. J., Gazzard, B. G., Griffiths, P. D., Jabs, D., Kern, E. R., Spector, S. A., & Whitley, R. J. (1998). Summary of the II International Symposium on Cytomegalovirus. *Antiviral Research, 39,* 141-162.

Delva, J., Bobashev, G., & Anthony, J. C. (2000). Clusters of drug involvement in Panama: Results from Panama's 1996 National Youth Survey. *Drug and Alcohol Dependence, 60,* 252–257.

Delva, J., & Castillo, M. (in press). International Research. In B. Thyer (Ed.), *Handbook of social work research methods* (2nd ed.). Thousand Oaks, CA: Sage Publications.

Delva, J., Spencer, M., & Lin, J. K. (2000). Racial/ethnic and educational differences in the estimated odds of recent nitrite use among adult household residents in the U.S.: An illustration of matching and conditional logistic regression. *Substance Use and Misuse, 35,* 269–290.

Delva, J., Tellez, M., Finlayson , T.L., Gretebeck, K.A., Siefert, K., Williams, D.R., & Ismail, A. (2005). Cigarette Smoking Among Low-Income African Americans:

A Serious Public Health Problem. *American Journal of Preventive Medicine, 29,* 218–220.

Delva, J., Tellez, M., Finlayson, T. L., Gretebeck, K. A., Siefert, K., Williams, D. R., & Ismail, A. I. (2006). Correlates of cigarette smoking among low-income African American women. *Ethnicity & Disease, 16,* 527–533.

Delva, J., Wallace, J. M., Bachman, J., O'Malley, P. M., Johnston, L. D., & Schulenberg, J. (2005). The epidemiology of alcohol, cigarettes, and illicit drugs among Mexican American, Puerto Rican, Cuban American, and other Latin American youths in the US: 1991–2002. *American Journal of Public Health, 95,* 696–702.

Denzin, N. K., & Lincoln, Y. (2000). *Handbook of qualitative research.* Thousand Oaks, CA: Sage Publications.

Dewey, J. (1933). *How we think: Restatement of the relation of reflective thinking to the educational process.* Washington, DC: Heath & Company.

Diamond, L. M., & Butterworth, M. (2008). Questioning gender and sexual identity: Dynamic links over time. *Sex Roles, 59,* 365-376.

Dillingham, B. (1977). Sterilization of Native Americans. *American Indian Journal, 3,* 16.

Donner, A., Birkett, N. & Buck, C. (1981). Randomization by cluster. *American Journal of Epidemiology, 114,* 906–914.

Dormitzer, C. M., Gonzalez, G. B., Penna, M., Bejarano, J., Obando, P., Sanchez, M., Vittetoe, K., Gutierrez, U., Alfaro, J., Meneses, G., Bolivar Diaz, J., Herrera, M., Hasbun, J., Chisman, A. M., Caris, L., Chen, C-Y., & Anthony, J. C. (2004). The PACARDO research project: youthful drug involvement in Central America and the Dominican Republic. *Pan American Journal of Public Health, 15,* 400–416.

Dowd, J. B., Aiello, A. E., & Alley, D. (2009). Socioeconomic disparities in the seroprevalence of cytomegalovirus infection in the U.S. population: National Health and Nutrition Examination Survey III. *Epidemiology and Infection, 137,* 58-65 1-8. DOI: 10.1017/S0950268808000551.

Dowd, J. B., Haan, M. N., Moore, K. A., Blythe, L., & Aiello, A. E. (2008). Socioeconomic gradients in immune response to latent infection. *American Journal of Epidemiology, 167,* 112–120.

Drisko, J. W. (2004). Qualitative data analysis software. In D. Padgett (Ed.), *The qualitative research experience* (p. 205). Belmont, CA: Wadsworth/Thomson Learning.

Dykeman, C., & Nelson, J. R. (1995). Building strong working alliances with American Indian families. *Social Work in Education, 17*(3), 148–58.

Fasenfest, D., & Gant, L. (2005). A model for ap-active and progressive university-community partnership. *Professional Development, 8*(2/3), 24–39.

Finlayson, T. L., Siefert, K., Ismail, A. I., Delva, J., & Sohn, W. (2005). Reliability and validity of brief measures of oral health-related knowledge, fatalism, and self-efficacy in mothers of African American Children. *Pediatric Dentistry*, *27*, 422–428.

Finn, J., & Jacobson, M. (2003). Just practice: *A social justice approach to social work*. Reosta, IA: Eddie Bowers Publishing, Inc.

Freire, P. (1970). *Pedagogy of the oppressed*. New York: Continuum.

Freligh, R. (2006). Sound Societies. *Leaders & Best*. Spring 2006.

Fukuyama, M. A. (1990). *Taking a universal approach to multicultural counseling. Counselor Education and Supervision, 30*, 6–25.

Gant, Larry (September 15, 2008) Personal Communication. Professor, School of Social Work, University of Michigan.

Gittelsohn, J., Steckler, A., Johnson, C., Pratt, C., Grieser, M., Picknel, J., Stone, E., Conway, T., Coombs, D., & Staten, L. (2008). Formative research in school and community-based health programs and studies: "State of the art" and the TAAG approach. *Health Education and Behavior, 33*, 25–39.

Good Tracks, J. G. (1973). Native American non-interference. *Social Work, 18*, 30–35.

Goodhart, F. W., Hsu, J., Baek, J. H., Coleman, A. L., Maresca, F. M., & Miller, M. B. (2006). A view through different lens: Photovoice as a tool for student advocacy. *Journal of American College Health, 55*, 53–56.

Gray, M., Yellow Bird, M., & Coates, J. (2008). Towards an understanding of indigenous social work. In M. Gray, J. Coates, & M. Yellow Bird (Eds.), *Indigenous social work around the world: Towards culturally relevant education and practice* (pp. 49–58). Burlington, VT: Ashgate.

Green, L. W., George, A., Daniel, M., Frankish, C. J, Herbert, C. P., Bowie, W. R., et al. (1995). *Study of participatory research in health promotion: Review and recommendations for the development of participatory research in health promotion in Canada*. Ottawa, Ontario, Canada: Royal Society of Canada.

Green, L. W., & Kreuter, M. W. (2005). *Health program planning: An educational and ecological approach*. New York: McGraw-Hill.

Grossman, Z., & McNutt, D. (2001). From enemies to allies: Native Americans and Whites join forces in Wisconsin. *Color Lines, Spring*, 22–25.

Guthrie, G. W., & Lonner, W. J. (1986). Assessment of personality and psychopathology. In W. J. Lonner & J. W. Berry (Eds.), *Field methods in cross-cultural research: Vol. 8. Cross cultural research and methodology series* (pp. 231–264). Beverly Hills, CA: Sage Publications.

Halfon, N., & Hochstein, M. (2002). Life course health development: An integrated framework for developing health, policy, and research. *The Milbank Quarterly, 80*, 433–479.

Hall, B., Gillete, A., & Tandon, R. (Eds.). (1982). *Creating knowledge: A monopoly?* Toronto, Ontario, Canada: International Council for Adult Education.

Hammersley, M., & Atkinson, P. (1996). *Ethnography: Principles in practice.* New York: Tavistock.

Harkness, J. A., Van de Vijver, F. J. R., & Mohler, P. Ph. (2003). *Cross-cultural survey methods.* Hoboken, NJ: Wiley.

Hawkins, J. D., Catalano, R. F., & Miller, J. Y. (1992). Risk and protective factors for alcohol and other drug problems in adolescence and early adulthood: Implications for substance abuse prevention. *Psychological Bulletin, 112,* 64–105.

Headland, T. N., Pike, K. L., & Harris, M. (Eds.). (1990). *Emics and etics: The insider/outsider debate.* Newbury Park, CA: Sage Publications.

Henle, W., & Henle, G. (1982). *Epstein-Barr virus and infectious mononucleosis.* In R. Glaser & T. Gottleib-Stematsky (Eds.), *Human herpes virus infections: Clinical aspects.* New York: Marcel Dekker.

Herbert, T., & Cohen, S. (1993). Stress and immunity in humans: A meta-analytic review. *Psychosomatic Medicine, 55,* 364–379.

Hick, S. (1997). Participatory research: An approach for structural social workers. *Journal of Progressive Human Services, 8*(2), 63–78.

Hodge, F. S., Fredericks, L., & Rodriguez, B. (1996). American Indian women's Talking Circles: A cervical cancer screening and prevention program. *Cancer, 78*(7), 1592–1597.

Horner, P., Sanchez, N., Castillo, M., & Delva, J. (2008, October). *Neighborhoods and drug use outcomes for Latin American youths.* Poster session presented at the Annual Meeting of the National Hispanic Science Network (NHSN) on Drug Abuse, Washington, DC.

Horner, P., Sanchez, N., Castillo, M., & Delva, J. (in press). Parental perceptions of neighborhood effects in Latino communities. *Substance Use & Misuse.*

Indian Gaming Regulatory Act, 25 U.S.C Sec. 2702 (1) (1988).

Israel, B. A., Krieger, J., Vlahov, D., Ciske, S., Foley, M., Fortin, P., et al. (2006). Challenges and facilitating factors in sustaining community-based participatory research partnerships: Lessons learned from the Detroit, New York City and Seattle urban research centers. *Journal of Urban Health: Bulletin of the New York Academy of Medicine, 83*(6), 1022–1040.

Israel, B. A., Schulz, A. J., Parker, E. A., & Becker, A. B. (1998). Review of community-based research: Assessing partnership approaches to improve public health. *Annual Review of Public Health, 19,* 173–202.

Jacobson, M., & Rugele, C. (2007). Community-based participatory research: Group work for social justice and community change. *Social Work with Groups, 30*(4), 21–39.

Jensen-DeHart, D. (1999, July 15). Casino helps poor tribe: Remote site supports reservation people. *Beloit Daily News,* 1–2.

Jezewski, M. A. (1990). *Culture brokering in migrant farm worker health care. Western Journal of Nursing Research, 12*(4), 497–513.

Jezewski, M. A., & Sotnik, P. (2001). *Culture brokering: Providing culturally competent rehabilitation services to foreign-born persons.* Retrieved October 5, 2008, from http://cirrie.buffalo.edu/monographs/cb.pdf

Joe, J. R. (1989). Values. In E. Gonzalez-Santin (Ed.), *Defining entry level competencies for public child welfare workers serving Indian communities* (pp.15–27). Tempe, AZ: O'Neil.

Johnson, B., & Christensen, L. (2004). *Educational research: Quantitative, qualitative, and mixed approaches.* Boston: Allyn & Bacon.

Johnston, L. D., O'Malley, P. M., Bachman, J. G., & Schulenberg, J. E. (2008). *Monitoring the future national survey results on drug use, 1975-2007. Volume I: Secondary school students* (NIH Publication No. 08-6418A). Bethesda, MD: National Institute on Drug Abuse.

Kennedy, S. (1996). Herpes virus infections and psychoneuroimmunology. In H. Friedman, T. Klein, & A. L. Friedman (Eds.), *Psychoneuroimmunology, stress, and infection* (pp. 231–242). New York: CRC Press.

Kim, K. H., Linnan, S., Campbell, M. K., Brooks C., Koenig, H. G., & Wiesen, C. (2008). The WORD (Wholeness, Oneness, Righteousness, Deliverance): A faith based weight-loss program utilizing a community-based participatory research approach. *Health Education and Behavior,* 35, 634–650.

Kish, L. (1965). Survey sampling. New York: John Wiley & Sons, Inc.

Koenig, H. G., Larson, D. B., & McCullough, M. E. (2001). *Handbook of religion and health.* New York: Oxford University Press.

Krieger, N. (2001). Theories for social epidemiology in the 21st century: An ecosocial perspective. *International Journal of Epidemiology, 30,* 668–677.

Krippendorff, K. (2004). *Content analysis: An introduction to its methodology* (2nd ed.). Thousand Oaks, CA: Sage Publications.

Krueger, R., & Casey, M. A. (2000). *Focus groups: A practical guide for applied research* (3rd ed.). Thousand Oaks, CA: Sage.

Kuh, D., & Ben-Schlomo, Y. (Eds.). (1997). *A life course approach to chronic disease epidemiology.* Oxford, England: Oxford University Press.

Lewin, K. (1946). *Action research and minority problems.* In G. W. Lewin (Ed.), *Resolving Social Conflicts* (pp. 201–216). New York: Harper & Row Publishers.

Love, A., & Muggah, B. (2005). Using democratic evaluation principles to foster citizen engagement and strengthen neighborhoods. *The Evaluation Exhange, 11*(3), 14–15.

Macaulay, A. C., Commanda, L. E., Freeman, W. L., Gibson, N., McCave, M. L., Robbins, C. M., & Twohig, P. L. (1998, November). *Responsible research with communities: Participatory research in primary care.* Policy statement presented at the NAPCRG Annual Membership Meeting, Montreal, Canada.

Maddux, J. E. (1995). *Self-efficacy, adaptation, and adjustment.* Theory, research, and application. New York: Plenum.

Garcia, F. M. (2000). Refereed research department: Warriors in education; persistence among American Indian doctoral recipients. Tribal College Journal of American Indian Higher Education, 11(2), 28Matsumoto, D. (1994). *Cultural influences on research methods and statistics.* Pacific Grove, CA: Brooks/Cole.

Maurrasse, D. J. (2001). *Beyond the campus: How colleges and universities form partnerships with their communities.* New York: Routledge.

Mehta, P. D., & West, G. (2000). Putting the individual back into individual growth curves. *Psychological Methods, 5,* 23–43.

Meredith, W., & Tisak, J. (1990). Latent curve analysis. *Psychometrika, 55,* 107–122.

Miller, W. R. (1983). Motivational interviewing with problem drinkers. *Behavioural Psychotherapy, 11,* 147–172.

Miller, P. (September 17, 2008) Personal Communication. School of Social Work, University of Michigan

Minkler, M., & Wallenstein, N. (2003). *Community-based participatory research for health.* San Francisco: John Wiley & Sons.

Mohatt, G. V., Hazel, K. L., Allen, J., Stachelrodt, M., Hensel, C., & Fath, R. (2004). Unheard Alaska: Culturally anchored participatory action research on sobriety with Alaska Natives. *American Journal of Community Psychology, 33*(3/4), 263–273.

Molloy, J. K. (2007). Photovoice as a tool for social justice workers. *Journal of Progressive Human Services, 18,* 39–55.

Momper, S. L., Delva, J., Reed, B. G. (in press). OxyContin abuse on a reservation: Qualitative reports by American Indians in Talking Circles. *Substance Use & Misuse.*

Momper, S. L., & Jackson, A. P. (2007). Maternal gambling, parenting, and child behavioral functioning in Native American families. *Social Work Research, 31*(4), 199–208.

Momper, S. L., & Nordberg, A. E. (2008, December). *Community collaborative research: students and residents as data collectors in a Detroit neighborhood health study.* Poster presented at the NIH Summit: The Science of Eliminating Health Disparities, Washington, DC.

Montejo, V. (1994). Oral tradition: Ancient words; oral tradition and the indigenous people of the Americas. *Native Americas, Fall/Winter,* 139.

Montero, M. (1994). Consciousness raising, conversion, and de-ideologization in community psychosocial work. *Journal of Community Psychology, 22*(1), 3–11.

Morgan, D. L. (2006). *Focus groups as qualitative research* (2nd ed.). Thousand Oaks, CA: Sage Publications.

Morgan, D. L., Fellows, C., & Guevara, H. (2008). Emergent approaches to focus group research. In S. Hesse-Biber & P. Leavy, (Eds.), *Handbook of emergent methods (pp. 189-207)*. New York City: Guilford Press.

Muthén, B. (2001). Second-generation structural equation modeling with a combination of categorical and continuous latent variables: New opportunities for latent class/latent growth modeling. In L. M. Collins & A. Sayer (Eds.), *New methods for the analysis of change* (pp. 291–322). Washington, DC: American Psychological Association.

Muthén, B., & Muthén, L. (2000). Integrating person-centered and variable-centered analysis: Growth mixture modeling with latent trajectory classes. *Alcoholism: Clinical and Experimental Research, 24,* 882–891.

Napoli, M. (1999). The non-Indian therapist working with the American Indian client: Transference and counter transference issues. *Psychoanalytic Social Work, 6*(1), 25–47.

National Survey of Student Engagement. (2008). Indiana University Center for Postsecondary Research. Bloomington, IN

Newcomb, M. D., Maddahian, E., & Bentler, P. M. (1986). Risk factors for drug use among adolescents: Concurrent and longitudinal analyses. *American Journal of Public Health, 76,* 525–531.

Orlandi, M. A., Weston, R., & Epstein, L. G. (Eds.). (1992). *Cultural competence for evaluators: A guide for alcohol and other drug abuse prevention practitioners working with ethnic/racial communities.* Rockville, MD: U.S. Department of Health and Human Services.

Pena, J. M., & Koss-Chioino, J. D. (1992). Cultural sensitivity in drug treatment research with African American males. In J. Trimble, C. S. Bolek, & S. J. Niemcryk (Eds.), *Ethnic and multicultural drug abuse: Perspectives on current research* (pp. 157–179). New York: The Haworth Press.

Pike, K. L. (1967). *Language in relation to a unified theory of the structure of human behavior* (2nd ed.). Berlin, Germany: Mouton De Gruyter.

Pinderhughes, E. (1989). Understanding race, ethnicity, and power: The key to efficacy in clinical practice. *Social Work, 39,* 314–323.

Prochaska, J. O., & DiClemente, C. C. (1983). Stages and processes of self-change of smoking: Toward an integrative model of change. *Journal of Consulting and Clinical Psychology, 51,* 390–395.

Raudenbush, S., Bryk, A., Cheong, Y. F., & Congdon, R. (2004). *HLM 6: Hierarchical linear and nonlinear modeling.* Lincolnwood, IL: Scientific Software International, Inc.

Red Horse, J. G. (1980). Family structure and value orientation in American Indians. *Social Work, 61,* 462–467.

Reise, S. P., Widaman, K. F., & Pugh, R. H. (1993). Confirmatory factor analysis and item response theory: Two approaches for exploring measurement invariance. *Psychological Bulletin, 114,* 552–566.

Resnicow, K., Braithwaite, R., Ahluwalia, J., & Baranowski, T. (1999). Cultural sensitivity in public health: Defined and demystified. *Ethnicity and Disease, 9*(1), 10–21.

Reynolds, W. M. (1982). Development of reliable and valid short forms of the Marlowe-Crowne Social Desirability Scale. *Journal of Clinical Psychology, 38,* 119–125.

Richards, L. (1999). Data alive! The thinking behind NVivo. *Qualitative Health Research, 9*(3), 88–93.

Rogler, L. H. (1989). The meaning of culturally sensitive research in mental health. *The American Journal of Psychiatry, 146*(3), 296–303.

Rollnick, S., & Miller, W. R. (1995). What is motivational interviewing? *Behavioural and Cognitive Psychotherapy, 23,* 325–334.

Rothman, J., & Epstein, I. I. (1977). Social planning and community organization: Social science foundations. In *Encyclopedia of social work* (17th ed., pp. 1433–1443). Washington, DC: National Association of Social Workers.

Sanchez, N., Delva, J., & Castillo, M. (2007, November). *Neighborhood characteristics and substance use among families: Differences between residents living on main streets and in passageways in Santiago, Chile.* Poster presented at Second Annual Global Health Symposium and Poster Session, Ann Arbor, Michigan.

Shanks, Trina (September 11, 2008) Personal communication. Assistant Professor, School of Social Work, University of Michigan.

Shields, S. A. (2008). Gender: An intersectionality perspective. *Sex Roles, 59,* 301–311.

Shulman, L. (2006). *The Skills of helping individuals, families, groups, and communities* (5th ed., pp. 269–278). Belmont, CA: Thomson Brooks/Cole.

Siefert, K., Finlayson, T. L., Williams, D. R., Delva, J., & Ismail, A. I. (2007). Modifiable risk and protective factors for depressive symptoms in low-income African American mothers. *American Journal of Orthopsychiatry, 77,* 113–123.

Stata Corporation. (2008). Stata 10 data analysis and statistical software. College Station, Texas: Author.

Steinman, K. J., & Zimmerman, M. A. (2004). Religious activity and risk behavior among African American adolescents: Concurrent developmental effects. *American Journal of Community Psychology, 33,* 151–161.

Storr, C. L., Chen, C-Y., & Anthony, J. C. (2004). "Unequal opportunity": Neighborhood disadvantage and the chance to buy illegal drugs. *Journal of Epidemiology and Community Health, 58,* 231–237.

Strack, R. W., Magill, C., & McDonagh, K. (2004). Engaging youth through Photovoice. *Health Promotion Practice, 5,* 49–58.

Strickland, J. C. (1999). Conducting focus groups cross-culturally: Experiences with Pacific Northwest Indian people. *Public Health Nursing, 16*(3), 190–197.

Stubben, J. D. (2001). Working with and conducting research among American Indian families. *American Behavioral Scientist, 44,* 1466–1481.

Swisher, K. (1996). Why Indian people should be the ones to write about Indian education. *The American Indian Quarterly, 20*(1), 83–90.

Tashakkori, A., & Teddlie, C. (2003). *Handbook of mixed methods in social and behavioral research.* Thousand Oaks, CA: Sage.

Tinkler, B. E., (2004). *Establishing a conceptual model of community-based research through contrasting case studies.* Retrieved October 8, 2008, from http://comm-org.wisc.edu/papers.htm

Triandis, H., Lambert, W., Berry, J., Lonner, W., Heron, A., Brislin, R., & Draguns, J. (Eds.). (1980). *Handbook of cross-cultural psychology:* Vols. 1-6. Boston: Allyn & Bacon.

United Nations Office on Drugs and Crime (UNODC) and the Inter-American Drug Abuse Control Commission (OAS/CICAD). (2006). *Youth and drugs in South American Countries: A public policy challenge: First comparative study of drug use in the secondary school student population in Argentina, Bolivia, Brazil, Colombia, Chile, Ecuador, Paraguay, Peru and Uruguay.* Retrieved January 10, 2009, from http://www.cicad.oas.org/oid/default.asp

United Native America (n.d.). *American Indian Holocaust.* Retrieved October 13, 2009, from http://www.unitednativeamerica.com/aiholocaust.html.

Volberg, R. A., & Abbott, M. A. (1997). Ethnicity and gambling: Gambling and problem gambling among indigenous peoples. *Substance Use and Misuse, 32*(11), 1525–1538.

Wang, C., & Burris, M. A. (1997). Photovoice: Concept, methodology, and use for participatory needs assessment. *Health Education and Behavior, 24,* 369–387.

Wang, C., & Burris, M. A. (2007). *Photovoice: Concept, methodology, and use for participatory needs assessment.* Abstract retrieved September 14, 2008, from http://www.ncbi.nlm.nih.gov/pubmed/9158980?dopt=Abstract

Wang, C., Morrel-Samuels, S., Hutchison, P. M., Bell, L., & Pestronk, R. M. (2004). Flint Photovoice: Community building among youths, adults, and policymakers. *American Journal of Public Health, 94,* 911–913.

Watson, D., Clark, L. A., & Tellegen, A. (1988). Development and validation of brief measures of positive and negative affect: The PANAS scales. *Journal of Personality and Social Psychology, 54,* 1063–1070.

Werner, E. E., & Smith, R. S. (2001). *Journeys from childhood to midlife.* Ithaca, NY: Cornell University Press.

Wetherington, C. L., Smeriglio, V. L., & Finnegan, L. P. (1996). Behavioral studies of drug-exposed offspring: Methodological issues in human and animal research (NIH Publication No. 96-4105). Rockville, MD: U.S. Department of Health and Human Services.

Willet, J. B., & Sayer, A. G. (1994). Using covariance structure analysis to detect correlations and predictors of individual change over time. *Psychological Bulletin, 116,* 363–381.

Wilson, N., Dasho, S., Martin, A. C., Wallerstein, N., Wang, C. C., & Minkler, M. (2007). Engaging young adolescents in social action through photovoice: The Youth Empowerment Strategies (YES!) project. *The Journal of Early Adolescence, 27*(2): 241–261.

Zajacova, A., Dowd J. B., Aiello, A. E. (2009). Socioeconomic and Racial/Ethnic Patterns in Persistent Infection Burden among U.S. adults. *The Journals of Gerontology: Biological Sciences and Medical Sciences, 64,* 272–279.

Ziedens, K., & McGee, K. (2006). *Planning phase I: Community goal and strategy areas.* University of Michigan, School of Social Work, Technical Assistance Center. Unpublished report.

Ziedens, K., & McGee, K. (2007). *Multi-level technical assistance strategy.* University of Michigan, School of Social Work, Technical Assistance Center. Unpublished report.

Zucker, R., Boyd, G., & Howard, J. (1994). *The development of alcohol problems: Exploring the biopsychosocial matrix of risk* (NIH Publication No. 94-3495). Rockville, MD: U.S. Department of Health and Human Services.

Index